MARCO POLO

Travel with
**Insider
Tips**

BANGKOK

MYANMAR   LAOS

THAI-
LAND

*South
China
Sea*

Andaman
Islands
(INDIA)

Bangkok

VIET-
NAM

CAMBODIA

INDIAN

OCEAN

INDON. MALAYSIA

I0620685

www.marco-polo.com

The best Insider Tips → p. 4

INSIDER TIP

Best of ... → p. 6

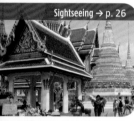

Sightseeing → p. 26

Food & Drink → p. 56

SYMBOLS

INSIDER TIP	Insider Tip
★	Highlight
●●●●	Best of ...
☼	Scenic view
🕙	Responsible travel: fair trade principles and the environment respected

PRICE CATEGORIES HOTELS

Expensive   over 2800 baht

Moderate   1600–2800 baht

Budget   under 1600 baht

The prices apply to a double room without breakfast. Single rooms are only nominally cheaper

PRICE CATEGORIES RESTAURANTS

Expensive   over 600 baht

Moderate   400–600 baht

Budget   under 400 baht

The prices apply per person for one main meal without drinks

On the cover: Awe-inspiring visit to the reclining Buddha p. 33 | Live concerts in Lumphini Park p. 41

CONTENTS

Shopping → p. 68

Entertainment → p. 80

Where to stay → p. 88

Street atlas → p. 118

DID YOU KNOW?

MAPS IN THE GUIDEBOOK

(120 A1) Page numbers and coordinates refer to the street atlas
(0) Site/address located off the map
Coordinates are also given for places that are not marked on the street atlas
Skytrain/Mass Rapid Transit (MRT) plan inside back cover

INSIDE BACK COVER: PULL-OUT MAP →

PULL-OUT MAP 𝄞

(𝄞 A–B 2–3) Refers to the removable pull-out map

The best MARCO POLO Insider Tips

Our top 15 Insider Tips

INSIDER TIP Dining out with a temple view
The Deck on the Chao Phraya River deserves its name: enjoy some delicious cuisine outdoors on the wooden deck overlooking the magnificent Wat Arun, the Temple of the Dawn, on the opposite river bank (photo above) → **p. 67**

INSIDER TIP Hip fashion at reasonable prices
Bangkok's fashion-conscious youth go shopping in the maze of alleyways in Siam Square. Designers here offer their latest designs at bargain prices → **p. 78**

INSIDER TIP Luxury need not be expensive
The rooms in the Apartment Hotel Grand President are equipped for comfort and even come with their own kitchenettes. You can relax in one of their three swimming pools, the sauna and in the spa. A stay here is excellent value for money → **p. 90**

INSIDER TIP Getting there is half the fun
In the middle of the metropolis is a pedestrian route that only a handful of people know about. Take an uninterrupted stroll past banana trees and a canal where monitors swim → **p. 51**

INSIDER TIP Riverside living
Stay at the Navalai River Resort and you will have the Chao Phraya right at your door and you can dine to the sound of lapping water at the Aquatini Restaurant → **p. 94**

INSIDER TIP Bangkok rocks
The Rock Pub is the address for those who love their music live and loud. Bands turn up the heat here and when Thailand's guitar legend, Lam Morrison, gets going the place is on fire → **p. 86**

INSIDER TIP Ironclad monastery
There are many monasteries in Bangkok but the Wat Ratnada is unique – its towers are made out of iron → **p. 55**

INSIDER TIP **In perfect harmony**
The Harmonique is a lovely little restaurant filled with antiques and traditional teahouse tables that serves Thai-Chinese home cooking made with the freshest ingredients → p. 65

INSIDER TIP **Alleyway action**
Sampeng Lane the bustling main alley in Bangkok's old Chinatown where business is booming and China is thriving (photo below) → p. 39

INSIDER TIP **Art and artists**
The Queen's Gallery offers established and aspiring Thai artists a platform, a large number of contemporary artworks on display → p. 37

INSIDER TIP **Among students**
The Phra Athit Road is Bangkok's Latin Quarter and it is where students from the nearby Thammasat University like to go out and party, there is always live music being played somewhere here → p. 83

INSIDER TIP **As colourful as life**
It's happened to be a Closet, not only is the name eccentric, but this boutique in the Emporium shopping centre sells both outrageous fashions and unusual delicacies like duck breast in plum sauce → p. 72

INSIDER TIP **Old Bangkok**
To experience what Bangkok was like 50 years ago take a stroll through Soi Sukha with its weathered wooden houses and traditional shops → p. 102

INSIDER TIP **Bob Marley forever**
The king of reggae would also have enjoyed the Brick Bar where live bands get foreign and local Rastafarians into the party mood → p. 84

INSIDER TIP **Grand Palace in miniature**
In the Rattanakosin Exhibition Hall you can marvel at a detailed model of the Grand Palace and learn all about the history of the city's oldest district → p. 37

BEST OF ...

GREAT PLACES FOR FREE
Discover new places and save money

● *A millionaire's garden*

A nice place to relax: *Chuvit Garden* off the hubbub of Sukhumvit Road is a private park that belongs to a wealthy man who doesn't charge an admission fee. The park is peaceful and atmospheric in the early evenings when the lanterns are lit → p. 46

● *Picture-perfect monastery*

Tourists have to pay an admission fee in Bangkok's most renowned temples but off the beaten track you can find wonderful monasteries that do not require a donation. The *Wat Bonwon Wiwet* is a peaceful oasis with ponds and exquisite murals → p. 38

● *Fitness and symphonies in the park*

You can get fit for free using the outdoor exercise equipment in *Lumphini Park* and for something a little less strenuous the Bangkok Symphony Orchestra offers concerts at no charge every Sunday from December to January. Why not take a picnic basket to the Concert in the Park! (photo) → p. 41

● *Designs from all over the world*

What is design? The answer can be found at the *Thailand Creative & Design Centre* where there are design exhibits from Thai and foreign designers from all fields and entrance is free. View international high-lights from the Vespa to the Barbie doll → p. 52

● *The King for free*

In the *King Prajadhipok Museum* you can learn everything about this unhappy ruler's life and a turbulent time in Thailand's political history. And unusually for Thai mu-seums, even tourists are allowed to enter without paying an admission fee → p. 51

● *Avant-garde art*

For a free insight into the current trends in the Thai art scene visit the *Bangkok Art and Culture Centre*. The futuristically-styled centre is an eye catcher → p. 46

 Dots in guidebook refer to 'Best of ...' tips

ONLY IN BANGKOK
Unique experiences

● *Life on a canal*

'Venice of the East' is no cliché: canals or *khlongs* spread throughout the *Thonburi* district like a giant spider web. Take a long-tail boat tour and see the old shingle-covered teak stilt houses → p. 53

● *Exquisite travesty*

You will see transvestites everywhere in Bangkok – the ladyboys are out and proud in this tolerant metropolis – and the most beautiful of them can be found at the *Calypso Cabaret*. Dressed in opulent outfits they give their audience an action-packed show → p. 86

● *The budget traveller*

The *Khao San Road* is loud, colourful and unique not only in Bangkok, but worldwide – and all the international backpackers meet here. Explore this iconic mile where a party takes place every night at the hippest bars → p. 82

● *Midnight snack*

Fast food on the pavement: Bangkok's street cooks prepare delicious snacks and even full meals right on the road. For the haute cuisine of street food go to *Soi 38 in Sukhumvit Road*, where they serve delicious gourmet food at midnight → p. 61

● *Palace of palaces*

Many royals had palaces built in Bangkok but none is grander than the *Grand Palace*. This fairy tale building with its Wat Phra Kaeo temple is an absolute must. It is an architectural testimony to the close bond between the Thai monarchy and Buddhism (photo) → p. 29

● *Tailor-made*

At first glance every second shop in Bangkok appears to be a tailor. But be warned: not everyone is a master of his trade. The ones offering tempting bargains and those with touts at the door are best avoided. A better bet would be to go to a reputable professional like *Pinky Tailor* → p. 79

ONLY IN

BEST OF ...

● **Siam's treasure chest**
The *National Museum* houses the treasures of the kingdom: jewellery, swords, Buddhas and much more. Free English tours, given by volunteers, are also available → p. 30

● **Skywalk to the shops**
Bangkok's most important shopping mile is on the Skytrain route and when it rains you can have direct access to the city's temples of commerce (photo), for example the massive shopping centre *Central World*. The covered Skywalk will keep you dry → p. 72

● **Noble art**
At the *National Art Gallery* you will see paintings, sculptures and works of art by well known artists as well as exhibitions of the artworks by the Thai monarchy → p. 36

● **Off to the aquarium**
When it rains why not take a dive – into the glass tunnels under the shark pool in the large *Siam Ocean World*. You can even find penguins here – in the middle of the tropics! → p. 105

● **At home with a silk king**
American Jim Thompson built up the Thai silk industry and collected artworks and antiques from Asia on the side. You can view this unique collection at *Jim Thompson House*, his previous residence, which in itself is a rarity → p. 48

● **Visit Madonna and friends**
What are Madonna and Brad Pitt doing together in Bangkok? They are waiting for visitors in *Madame Tussauds* wax museum. You probably won't know the Thai celebrities, but all the other sculptures are global celebrities → p. 47

RAIN

○●●○ Dots in guidebook refer to 'Best of ...' tips

RELAX AND CHILL OUT
Take it easy and spoil yourself

● *Wellness*

Feel like Cleopatra and try a milk bath at *Health Land* where your spa dreams become reality – and at refreshingly low prices. The spa chain spoils its guests with superb services in luxurious wellness oases. You will feel like royalty after a two-hour Thai massage or their Royal Thai Package → **p. 32**

● *Heavenly cocktails*

The *Sky Bar* in *The Dome* is an ultra modern venue in glass that is lit from the inside in neon blue. With a flute of champagne in hand you can enjoy the glittering city at your feet – heavenly. The 220m/720ft high rooftop restaurant *Sirocco* offers Bangkok's best gastronomy → **p. 63**

● *Sweet temptations*

Pralines, tarts, cakes – Bangkok's sweet temptations in the bakeries of the shopping centre *Emporium* will ruin any diet → **p. 72**

● *Massage in a monastery*

Exhausted from hours of sightseeing? A massage in a monastery loosens up the muscles and helps tired tourists back on their feet. In the *Wat Pho* at the Grand Palace the masters of this art are at work as this is where Thailand's most famous massage school is located → **p. 33**

● *Calming lake*

Time to take a deep breath and stroll on the promenade around the lake in *Benjakiti Park* near the tourist mile Sukhumvit Road. There is lots of calming green and a view of the distant skyscrapers and you can go at your own pace in one of the paddle boats → **p. 50**

● *Dinner on the deck*

A dinner cruise on the Chao Phraya in the luxurious *Apsara* barge is a delight for the senses: the glittering lights of the big city, the wine at just the right temperature, the finest food (photo) and a light breeze blowing over the river → **p. 61**

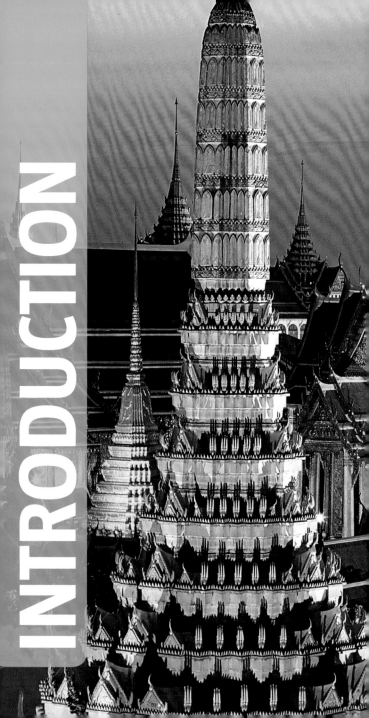

INTRODUCTION

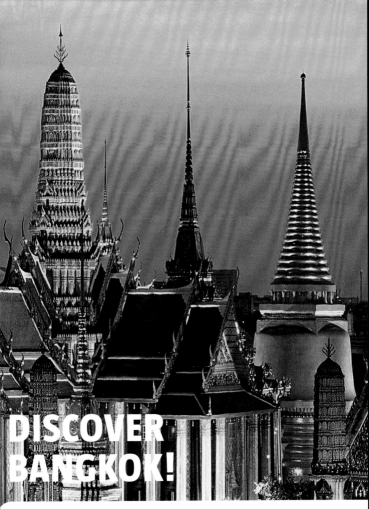

DISCOVER BANGKOK!

Bangkok between heaven and earth: on the rooftops of skyscrapers top chefs create gourmet meals in the hippest restaurants while down below mobile cooks fry up marinated meat on charcoal fires on the pavements. Bangkok between speed and leisure: a lightning fast underground train zooms through the city while a vegetable seller paddles from house to house on quiet canals.

Bangkok between bargains and luxury, parties and faith: you can get T-shirts for the price of a bottle of beer at the open air markets, while the glitzy shopping centres offer the latest designer handbags that cost more than a university professor earns in a month. International DJs play the latest tracks in the stylish clubs, whilst monks sink deep into in meditation in the city's monasteries.

Photo: Wat Phra Kaeo

Bangkok is not just another large city; Bangkok is a universe in itself. Typically Thai on the one hand yet very cosmopolitan on the other. A city that unifies a traditional past with a modern life, one that captures the past and anticipates the future.

Welcome to contemporary Bangkok, a metropolis of contrasts! In other words: Bangkok is characterised by the interplay of constantly changing tensions. Especially since the beginning of the new millennium, change has been rapidly progressing as the city reaches for the stars. The apartment towers on the Chao Phraya River are becoming higher and higher, the shopping centres bigger and more elegant and Bangkok is becoming trendier by the day. In the space of a few years Thailand's capital city has become South East Asia's design and fashion stronghold. Thai fashion labels are conquering the international catwalks. Boutique hotels with their individually deco-rated rooms are attracting style-conscious globetrotters and architects are designing futuristic high-rise buildings, like the Hotel Centara Grand that could be a backdrop for a fantasy film, with its sky-blue dome.

At first glance Bangkok is pure chaos

At first glance Bangkok is pure chaos: multiple-lane motorways cut through the cityscape, concrete buildings and traffic-jammed streets shape the scenery. Crowds stream between hawkers and fast food stalls on the pavements and have to dodge the moped drivers who use the pavement as a shortcut. The Thais are used to the chaos. 'Mai pen rai', they say: 'it doesn't matter'. You will need to keep your cool to survive in Bangkok; your nerves will be

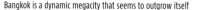

Bangkok is a dynamic megacity that seems to outgrow itself

tested. Perhaps you will have the same reaction as many other visitors have when they first visit the capital city: they immediately want to leave this mayhem, as it seems as if there is no part that they can retreat to. There is no actual centre, no clear differentiation between residential and business districts. Everything is everywhere and all at the same time! But any visitor to the city will soon find out that, despite its chaos, Bangkok is a city of happy people, a city of joy and smiles. And if you look behind the modern western façade, you will also discover that Bangkok is still full of exotic tradition.

Dawn does not last long in the tropics and as soon as the sun rises over the low horizon, the traffic jams begin. A taxi is stuck on a bridge over a *khlong*, the driver drums his thumb on the steering wheel in frustration. Then he pauses and smiles apologetically. He turns his eyes to the water, to an old woman in a wooden boat. She is paddling with short strokes, gliding effortlessly ahead. Now the driver is grinning. He

> Despite the confusion, this is a city of smiles

knows that if modern Bangkok disappeared in a flash; it would not be a tragedy. According to the teachings of Buddha, nothing in this life lasts. Raindrops turn to oceans, oceans to raindrops it is all part of a never-ending cycle. The Thais would simply return to using the paddle.

By around 1900 there were about half a million people living in the capital of what was then Siam. Bangkok was already a large city, not a metropolis, but rather a collec-

tion of villages where artisans and their families lived. Rice mills and sawmills lined the Chao Phraya, Thailand's longest river, which flows straight through the centre of the metropolis. Most of the houses were made out of wood with only a few commercial and government buildings, temples and palaces built out of stone. That is why this young city only has a handful of private buildings that are hundred years or older. Even though the first car to rattle through Bangkok arrived as early as 1897, there were only a few stretches of paved road.

This was because the river and canals formed the most important traffic routes. This was not without danger as crocodiles were still swimming in the Chao Phraya in 1900. Those who dared to catch one were given a reward by the local authorities. Early travellers from the West described

Bangkok as the 'Venice of the East', a floating city where its children grew up with a paddle in their hands.

Many of the original canals have long since been filled in or changed into roads. But Thonburi still has a network of waterways. If you charter a boat yourself and leave the main thoroughfares and explore the areas that are too shallow for the tourist boats you will be rewarded with the Bangkok of old. Palms cast their shadows on the shingle-covered stilt houses along the green banks; an old lady cooks rice on a stove, which looks like a perforated flowerpot, a vegetable vendor paddles a boat filled with baskets of garlic, chillies, tomatoes and cucumbers. On a jetty a monk meditates in an orange-coloured robe. And a few metres away children are splash in the water. Even in fast-paced Bangkok there are still areas of peace and calm.

A lot has changed since 1782, when King Rama I moved the capital of Siam from Thonburi to the rather minor village of Bangkok on the other side of the Chao Phraya. He named the new capital Krung which means 'city of angels'. Even though Bangkok is the international name used, the Thais still call their capital by its nicer name. Today the capital is by far the most important business centre in the country. Half of the country's gross domestic product is earned in the greater Bangkok area and the city is a magnet for jobs seekers and rural migrants. According to statistics, nearly eight million people live in the capital, but no one knows the exact number of inhabitants. This is because a large number come from the poor provinces, specifically from the drought-affected north-east, but continue to be registered as residents of their home towns.

And so Bangkok has continued to expand both on the ground and upwards with its skyscrapers. When the Hotel Dusit Thani was opened in 1970, its 23 floors made it giant on the city's skyline. At the time the city's sceptics said that buildings should not go any higher and pointed to research that claimed that the capital was sinking a little every year. Today a forest of high-rise buildings looms over the smog of the city. The 88-floor Baiyoke Sky Hotel (309m/1010ft) is the highest building in Thailand and it completely dwarfs the Dusit Thani.

Every morning an offering to the spirits

Bangkok is also the cultural and religious centre of Thailand. About 95 per cent of Thais are Buddhists and follow the teachings of Siddhartha Gautama, known as Buddha. However, many still also believe in the spirit world and to prevent the spirits from roaming about restlessly, a little house has to be built for them. Usually the house is no bigger than a birdhouse and stands on a pole in the garden, or in the entrance area or parking lot. Every morning without fail, this invisible neighbour will be given offerings; flowers, rice, a glass of water, incense. This spirituality controls everyday life in Bangkok just like the rush hour on the Menam Chao Phraya, one of the city's largest thoroughfares.

Visitors to Bangkok will soon smell the city's typical 'aroma' created by the fumes of buses, clattering tuk-tuks and countless cars and motorbikes. Traffic jams are the order of the day at the junction of the multi-laned main streets of Ploenchit, Rama I and Ratchadamri, everything grinds to a halt. But high over the junction things are different with the elevated electric railway line: the Skytrain. But

> **The scent of incense overlays the clouds of exhaust fumes**

even here, at this urban nightmare of a crossing, Bangkok is different from every other city with traffic problems. Here the smell of incense masks the clouds of exhaust

Bangkok was built on the water: take an express boat on the Chao Phraya

fumes and Thai classical music penetrates through the sounds of trilling whistles and car alarms. And even the graceful dancers in their glittering ceremonial costumes are not a figment of your imagination. They dance around the gilded statue of the Hindu god Brahma at the Erawan Shrine. The intersection shrine draws construction workers and bankers alike to worship while barmaids kneel down next to housewives with lotus flowers in their folded hands.

Of course Bangkok has many attractions that are a must-see for tourists. However, to discover life in all its diversity you should mingle with the Thai people themselves. Dive into the noisy maze of the markets, and then catch your breath in a wat, one of the city's 400 monasteries. Visit one of the ostentatious shopping centres, then glide in a boat on a canal where time seems to stand still. It is these contrasts that make up the true Bangkok.

WHAT'S HOT

1 Art cafés

Art awakening In *The Anna* not only can you eat well, but you can also enjoy the art on display in the adjoining gallery *(27 Soi Piphat, Satorn Nua Rd, www.theanna restaurant.com, photo)*. In *Dicks Café* gastronomy and art also go hand in hand with displays of temporary exhibits by regional artists *(Duangthawee Plaza, 894/7–8 Soi Pratoochai, Surawong Rd, www.dickscafe.com)*. The *Chalit Art Project* is an art school with a gallery and a place of inspiration for many aspiring artists *(Ratchawithi Rd, Soi 2)*.

Well dressed 2

Local Designers Perfect for the urban look are the designs by *Greyhound (Siam Centre, Unit 340-341, 3rd floor, www.greyhound.co.th, photo)* and for a super-feminine look try the designs by *Fly Now Bangkok (www.flynowbangkok.com)*. The search for local fashion labels will also lead you straight to the malls; *Emporium (Sukhumvit Rd, Soi 24, www.emporium thailand.com)* and *Siam Paragon (Rama I Rd, www. siamparagon.co.th)*.

Spa special

Spa-party Instead of meditation music Bangkok's spa visitors now get to experience something new. The *Bangkok Oasis Spa* takes care of its wellness guests with good music, healthy drinks and relaxation programmes *(31 Su-khumvit Rd, Soi Sawasdee 64, www.bangkokoasis.com)* while at the *Lullaby Spa* you will be soothed into a state of relaxation *(Q House Lumpini Building, 1 Satorn Tai Rd, www.lullaby-spa. com)*, or you can also try the *Leyana Spa (33 Thong-lor 13, Soi Torsak, Klongton-Nue, Wattana, www.leyanaspa.com)*.

Healthy eating

Food trend Thai cuisine has lots of healthy ingredients, but now the major cities are going one better. Organic and vegan food is now also being served in the trendy restaurants. The *Rasayana Café* specialises in raw food – you must try their vegetable drink *(57 Soi Prommitr, 39 Sukhumvit Rd, www.rasayanaretreat.com)*! In *Healthy Spice* special attention has been given to the healing effects of herbs and spices *(434 Yan Phahon-yothin Rd, Chatu-chak)*. In *Glow* you even go one step further. The menu is sorted by enzymes, vitamins and minerals so each guest can put together their own individual meal *(The Metropolitan Bangkok, 27 Satorn Tai Rd, www.metropolitan.bangkok.como.bz, photo)*.

Bangkok by night

Nightlife The evening begins with a ride in a karaoke taxi. From the outside it looks like completely normal taxi, but inside the booming bass and the light show sets the atmosphere. Finding one on the street is difficult, so best order one through your hotel. Next up your drive takes you to a house in the form of a beer keg, the *Tawan Dang*. This restaurant and bar is well known for its home-brewed beers and stage shows. This is where Thai and Western influences meet and the results are amusing, inspiring and sometimes downright odd *(462/61 Rama III Rd, www.tawandang.com)*. Those who don't feel like going home after closing time can move on to the mobile bars of Sukhumvit Road where tuk-tuks are magically transformed into tables and chairs in one swift move of the hand.

IN A NUTSHELL

BEGGARS

There are as many beggars in Bangkok as in any other large metropolitan city. However, in Bangkok the beggars prefer to ask for handouts in area where there are lots of tourists. At times you may see a mother with a baby, or small children with puppies, or cripples with dirty bandages. Begging is a tough business controlled by gangs who operate behind the scenes.

ELEPHANTS

You may think you are hallucinating when you see an elephant in the middle of Bangkok. Their drivers, the mahouts, bring these grey giants into the capital city in trucks. Once in the city they take them begging, usually in the tourist areas. You can purchase bananas from the mahout and then feed the elephants but by doing this you are not actually helping the elephants. As long as the men make a profit, the elephants will be continue to be driven through Bangkok, even if it is against council bylaws. A large city with its noise, exhaust fumes and the hot tarred roads is a no place an elephant and they often fall ill.

FASHION

Fashion in Bangkok has changed and now there is far more to it than the

Photo: Mask dance

Spirit houses are everywhere and don't be surprised if your taxi is overtaken by an elephant

bargain, mass-produced printed T-shirts sold on every street corner. In the large shopping malls luxury boutiques offer the latest outfits from the style capitals of the world, from Paris to Tokyo. But Thai fashion designers can also hold their heads up high with well-established labels like Flynow and Greyhound creating an international sensation. And there are a number of young designers are mixing it up with some very creative designs. If you would like to see what the next trendsetters' hit will be, then take a stroll through the Chatuchak Weekend Market. This gigantic flea market showcases the latest designs by Bangkok's avant-garde designers. And the shopping centres you can often see fashion shows with models presenting Thai designs.

LOCAL CUSTOMS

Thais are tolerant people and seldom interfere in the affairs of others and especially not in those of foreigners. This means that tourists do enjoy a certain amount of freedom but this does not extend to offending the royal family. Buddhism, its followers and symbols should also be treated with respect. You need to remove your shoes when entering temples (but not Chinese temples), mosques and private homes. Women are not allowed to touch monks or sit next to them on the bus. Take care to wear suitable clothing when visiting temples or official buildings (no flip-flops, shorts, skirts, or sleeveless blouses). Otherwise you may not be allowed to enter, or you will be allowed in but then you may not be served. They are particularly strict about what you wear at The Grand Palace but you can also rent shoes or a robe once you are there. Thais show no regard for a person who shows his anger openly and loss of self-control is deplored by the Thais. Some Westerners mistakenly believe that the Thais considers their heads to be sacred, in fact the Thais do consider the head to be the highest body part, literally and figuratively. So, as a foreigner, you should not touch the head of a local, even if you mean it in a friendly manner. On the other hand, the lowest part of the body, the sole of the foot should never be shown to others.

MASK DANCE

An important aspect of the Asian cultural arena is the Indian epic the *Ramayana*. It is the story of Prince Rama's odyssey, how he rescues his wife Sita from a demon. The Thai version is called *Ramakien* and scenes from this story form the backdrop for the magnificent costume parade *Khon*. The Thai masked dance is a theatrical art of motion with slow motion pieces where every gesture conveys a certain emotion. The cast of the drama remain silent, narrators tell the story and the orchestra provides the musical frame. You can watch *Ramakien* performances at the National Theatre and in the Sala Chalemkrung Royal Theatre. Occasionally hotels do their own versions of *Khon* at dinner shows. You can find schedules in the city's newspapers, the 'Bangkok Post' or 'The Nation'.

MEDICAL TOURISM

Holiday and a hospital visit? In Bangkok medical tourism is booming and not only because many doctors have specialised in cosmetic procedures. Most Thai doctors are educated in Europe or the US; the prices for treatment and operations are far cheaper than in the West and the hospitals are of an international standard and care for patients from all over the world. South East Asia's largest private clinic, the Bumrungrad, has more than 400,000 patients per year. Numerous dentists also cater to foreign visitors and it need not be pain that sends you to the dentist in Bangkok. An oral hygiene session costs about 800 baht. The state tourism board has even opened its own website for medicinal tourism *(www.thailand medtourism.com)*.

NIGHTLIFE

Clichés remain entrenched and many people still associate Bangkok with sex tourism. But the city has transformed into an international metropolis and has undergone obvious changes. These can be seen in the modern high rise buildings, the shopping centres and in the dramatic change in its nightlife. Yes, they do still exist, the bars where the bikini girls dance around chrome poles, and the cheap beer bars that are no more than an open air huts. But there are less and less of them and in the red light district the infamous Patpong is closing down go-go bars and reopening them as chic lounges or as souvenir shops. Up-and-coming stylish clubs like those in Berlin or New York are on the rise and the real trend is for rooftop bars on high-rise buildings. Whether simple or chic: in Bangkok all the lights and speakers are turned off in the nightclubs selves as the guardians of the country and monarchy and have overthrown a number of unpopular governments, most recently in 2006 against Prime Minister Thaksin who was accused of corruption. There have been repeated demonstrations by supporters of the exiled Thaksin, most of who are from the poorer classes. In 2008 Thaksin's opponents occupied the airport for days

Cool space-age interior: a visit to Bangkok's Bed Supperclub is an absolute must

at two in the morning. Closing hours are strictly adhered to. However, the city manages to keep going thereafter as there are mobile bars on the pavements that offer drinks bargains after closing time.

POLITICS

Parliamentary democracy in Thailand is on shaky ground because the real power lies with the military. They see themand thousands of tourists could not leave the country. In 2010 the military and police violently broke up a protest of Thaksin supporters who occupied a central crossing in Bangkok's most important shopping district for weeks. Dozens of people died and the foreign media in particular reported that civil war was imminent but Bangkok quickly returned to normality. However, the reasons behind the unrest and violent conflicts over the last years remain unresolved. An ever-increasing middle class is seeking a political voice, and even the rural poor want to have their needs met.

PRICES

As a foreigner you may experience a different price structure than the locals, this is a bone of contention and constant topic in the readers' columns in the 'Bangkok Post' and 'The Nation'. Many private attractions like Madame Tussauds wax museum charge foreigners a higher admission fee (850 baht) than the locals (350 baht). And even at royal places of interest like the Vimanmek Royal Palace Zoo tourists (100 baht) must pay more than the locals (75 baht). Not all visitors are equal, even before Buddha: foreigners have to pay an admission fee at temples while the Thai may enter for free. This also applies when you bargain at markets or will a tuk-tuk driver. Most of the Thai see this system of different pricing as a kind of compensatory justice: they simply assume that tourists have more money than they do.

ROYAL FAMILY

Even though Thailand has not been an absolute monarchy since 1932, the royal family is still regarded very highly. The Thais do not take lightly to disrespectful remarks about their royal family and an insult to the monarchy is a punishable offence and it also applies to tourists. An example would be that if the national anthem plays before a movie in the cinema, the Thais also expect any foreigners to stand up.

SPELLING VARIATIONS

Are you, the white foreigner, a *falang* or a *farang?* Would you like to travel further to Ko Samui or Koh Samui? *Ko(h)* means

island, but why are there two spellings? Why do you sometimes write *hat* for beach and sometimes *had* and sometimes *haad?* Newcomers often ask these questions but there are no clear answers. Thai writing is a closed book, written in graceful yet illegible squiggles and there are no clear rules on how to translate them into Latin characters.

SPIRIT HOUSES

You may not see spirits in Bangkok, but you will find their houses everywhere. There are spirit houses *(ban)* in front of businesses and shopping centres, apartments and banks. The shrines resemble miniature temples, but have nothing to do with Buddhism. The Thais' belief in spirits *(phi)* is deeply rooted. They bring

Wat Pho is the oldest and largest Buddhist temple monastery in the capital

daily offerings to these invisible neighbours to honour and calm them so that they will not get up to any mischief. The offerings include incense, bowls of rice, fruit or even cans of cola. On important days the spirits may even receive a roast chicken! Many pedestrians show their respect by putting their hands together as they walk past the shrine. The largest and most famous spirit house in the city is the Erawan Shrine where thousands of devotees visit on a daily basis.

WAT

This is the name for a temple and monastery complex. Usually the temple and monastery belong together but an exception is the Wat Phra Kaeo in the Grand Palace. This royal palace has no adjoining monastery. The prayer hall of a wat is called a *bot. Chedi* are the tapered bell-shaped towers while the tall towers in classical the Khmer-style are called *prang*.

WELLNESS

Bangkok is the massage capital of the world. No, there is nothing disreputable about that as we are not talking about brothels that disguise themselves as massage salons, but wellness oases where body and spirit can relax. Luxurious spas can be found throughout the city and are not only limited to the top hotels *(www.thaiwebsites.com/spas.asp)*. There are simple massage salons, where you can receive an hour-long massage for about 400 baht, on almost every street corner.

THE PERFECT DAY
Bangkok in 24 hours

07:30am BREAKFAST WITH A RIVER VIEW

A breakfast at *Aquatini* will get you into the flow of a perfect day in Bangkok. The terrace restaurant of the Hotel *Navalai River Resort* → p. 94 is a vantage point with a view over the Chao Phraya. If you like typical Thai food first thing in the morning then try a *kao tom gai*, a spicy rice soup with chicken served with a lightly beaten egg.

08:30am GRAND PALACE & A FOOT MASSAGE

The middle of old Bangkok provides the perfect setting for a stroll to some the main places of interest. Walk downstream via Phra Athit Road and Rachini Road to *Sanam Luang* → p. 31 (photo left) the tamarind tree-lined area in front of the *Grand Palace* → p. 29. This route also leads to the *National Museum* → p. 30, where you can marvel at Siam's treasures. Bangkok's real architectural jewel is of course the palace itself with the royal temple *Wat Phra Kaeo* → p. 29. Right next to it is the most famous monastery in the country, *Wat Pho* → p. 33. And if your feet are aching, there is a massage school to massage your pain away.

00:30pm WATERWAYS IN THONBURI

Over the river and into the water labyrinth: at the Tha Chang pier just to the right of the Grand Palace you can charter a long-tail boat. On the other side of Chao Phraya, the district of *Thonburi* → p. 53 is made up of a web of canals *(khlongs)* where you can discover a floating world with vegetable sellers paddling along and wooden stilt houses. On your way back a short detour to *Wat Arun* → p. 54 (photo right) with its 79m/260ft high *prang* riverbank landmark.

02:00pm BOAT TRIP & SHOPPING

You can quickly get into the flow of modern Bangkok: step onto the *Chao Phraya Tourist Boat* at the Tha Chang pier. A tour guide will explain the many sights, from temples through to churches and colonial buildings. The final stop is the King Taksin Bridge. From there you can take the Skytrain to Siam Central station and the hub of Bangkok's shopping area with its massive emporiums like the *Siam Centre* → p. 73 and the *Siam Paragon* → p. 73.

Get to know some of the most dazzling, exciting and relaxing facets of Bangkok – all in a single day

02:45pm **SHARKS & FISH DISHES**

Are there sharks in the middle of the city? Yes: in the *Siam Ocean World* → p. 105 in Siam Paragon. Or if you would rather eat fish then there are numerous fast-food restaurants in Siam Paragon *Food Hall* (on the ground floor).

04:15pm **ASIAN TREASURES**

Well fed you can now take the Skytrain (station Siam, access via Paragon) for a short trip to the Station National Stadium. From here it is only a few minutes away to the *Jim Thompson House* → p. 48 (photo) with its fascinating collection of Asian objects d'art.

05:15pm **THE BACKPACKER MILE**

There is also a lot to see on the *Khao San Road* → p. 35. Take a taxi to the mile that attracts backpackers from all over the world since the film 'The Beach' (with Leonardo DiCaprio) made it famous. The street is even crazier live than in the movies – a fantastic mix of freak show and flea market.

06:30pm **ROOFTOP COCKTAILS**

Now it is time for a sundowner – and it certainly tastes better in lofty heights. In the *Sky Bar* at the very top of *The Dome* → p. 62 the city lies at your feet. At heights of 220m/720ft your champagne cocktail will have some extra bubbles! And their dinner under the night sky is a feast for the senses. But you will definitely need reserve your table at *Sirocco* beforehand.

08:30pm **HEAD START IN THE NIGHT LIFE**

The bar street *Patpong* → p. 82 is only five minutes away by taxi but there are more souvenir shops than bars so the trendier option is a few minutes further in Soi 4 of Silom Road. And where do Bangkok's stylish clubbers go to? Two top destinations that have international DJs are the *Q Bar* → p. 85 and the *Bed Supperclub* → p. 84.

Boat at the starting point: Chao Phraya Express
Landing: Phra Athit Pier
For taxis: ask the hotel to write down your destination address in Thai!

SIGHTSEEING

CITY WHERE TO START?

Sanam Luang (120 B4–5) *(◻ B3):* The ideal point from which to start your exploration of the historical centre: The Grand Palace, Wat Pho, the National Museum and the Khao San Road are all within walking distance. At Wat Pho there are boats across to Wat Arun, while the ferries to Chinatown and further on to King Taksin Bridge, leave from the pier behind the Grand Palace. *Buses 503, 508, 511, MRT: Hua Lamphong, Skytrain: National Stadium*

Your first glance at a Bangkok street map may inspire a little fear: how are you meant to orientate yourself in this enormous city that covers a vast area over 620mi²?

But fear not! You can give the outskirts, with their residential suburbs and industrial areas, a miss. The Bangkok that is of interest to the tourist is contained in a manageable area that includes the sister city Thonburi in the West which is separated from Bangkok by the Chao Phraya River. If you would like to visit Thonburi, it is best to take a boat or the Skytrain as there are constant rush hour traffic jams on the bridges.

Photo: Wat Phra Kaeo

Palaces, parks and temples: discover fascinating places and havens of calm in the urban jungle of Bangkok

Bangkok itself is criss-crossed by multi-laned motorways and main roads. Branching off from the main streets are a network of side streets *(soi)* which are usually named and numbered by the main street that they lead off from. An example: Sukhumvit Road, Soi 11 is the 11th soi that branches off from Sukhumvit Street. Bigger sois have their own names. You should not just set off in Bangkok, you should rather plan your sightseeing tour – if you are staying in the tourist district in Sukhumvit Road and want to go to the historic old town, you will need a good three hours. Public transport will take you to all the city's sights.

If you take a bus, you should make sure you have coins and small notes. Most of the taxi drivers cannot speak English so have your hotel write down your desired

The map shows the location of the most interesting districts. There is a detailed map of each district on which each of the sights described is numbered.

destination in Thai. This is especially important when you want to visit one of the museums that are not that popular among the Thais. The Mass Rapid Transit (MRT) and the Skytrain (BTS) are both lightning fast and very clean. On the Skywalk, a walkway under the tracks, you can walk from Chit Lom station to Siam Central without going down onto the street and branches lead to the shopping centres.

RATTANA-KOSIN

The historic heart of the city beats in Rattanakosin, the old town in the bend of the Chao Phraya River.

King Rama I founded the city on the eastern bank of the Chao Phraya in a strategic location. Here the river makes a wide bend that forms a natural moat. To protect the city further east, the king built a city wall and had a canal dug, which led to the formation of the Rattanakosin peninsula. This is where you will find the most important tourist attractions: the Grand Palace, Wat Pho and the National Museum. Here you will also find ancient whitewashed buildings that house ministries and battered shop fronts that are home to both extended families and their businesses. While on the pavements at the Wat Mahathat and outside Thammasat University, hawkers sell charms and amulets. The entire area has been declared a national monument.

Nothing new has been built here and as such Rattanaskosin is a must for all who are interested in the history and culture of the city and the country, and for all who want to see the Bangkok of old. *MRT: Hua Lampong | Skytrain: National Stadium, from there about 15 minutes by taxi | Aircon buses no. 503 and 508 from Sukhumvit Rd across Rama I Rd to Grand Palace | Saen Saep khlong boat: Tha Phanfa (at the Golden Mount), from there about 15 minutes by foot | Chao Phraya express boats: Tha Tian, Tha Chang Luang, Tha Phra Chan*

■1 GRAND PALACE AND WAT PHRA KAEO ★ ●
(120 A–B 5–6) (*Ɯ B 3–4*)

Behind 1900m/6200ft long, crenulated walls are the Royal Palace and the Wat Phra Kaeo, the temple of the Emerald Buddha. They are the most famous attractions in Thailand – not only for tourists but for the Thai. The ensemble of buildings looks like they are straight out of a fairy tale. Colourful murals and paintings detail what life must have been like in the court. They tell the story of the *Ramakien*, the Thai epic about the battle between good and evil, and they depict details of Buddha's life. Outsized statues of graceful mythical creatures and rainbow-coloured demons stand guard over the complex. Delicate towers and golden *chedi*, tapered round towers, sweep heavenwards.

The central masterpiece is the Royal Temple with the most revered Buddha statue in the country, the legendary Emerald Buddha. It was discovered in 1434 in northern Thailand and was originally hidden under plaster which slowly crumbled to reveal the shimmering green Buddha beneath. In truth it is not made of emerald, but of jade, and at only 75cm is considered a national treasure that is reputed to have miraculous powers.

The structures that make up the Royal Palace were built in both the classic Thai and the Victorian style. The palace itself is only used for official occasions (the royal family now resides in Chit Lada Palace). Only those tourists who are appropriately dressed are allowed entry. Women should wear knee-length skirts or longer and should not wear sleeveless blouses, men must wear long pants. Even open sandals are frowned upon and it won't make any difference to point out that the Thais can go in wearing flip-flops. Shoes and robes can be hired at the entrance. *Daily 8.30am– 4.30pm, entrance until 3.30pm | admission fee 350 baht (the ticket also allows a visit to the Royal Mint and decoration collection in the palace grounds as well as admission to Vimanmek Royal Palace at Ratchawithi Rd) | only point of entry Na Phralan Rd | www.palaces.thai.net*

■2 LAK MUANG (120 B5) (*ω B3*)
The the city's foundation stone was laid by King Rama I. The stone is on display in a shrine that looks like a small temple. Visitors can paste gold leaf onto it, lay flowers or light candles and incense. Classic Thai dances are performed daily. *Ratchadamnoen Nai Rd (near the front of the Grand Palace at Sanam Luang)*

■3 NATIONAL MUSEUM ★ ●
(120 A–B4) (*ω B2*)
Founded in 1926 the National Museum is housed in a palace that is over 200 years old. The fantastic collection of artefacts traces Thailand's history back to prehistoric times. Ancient earthenware pots, the ornate thrones of the kings and gold-decorated royal hearses and swords used in battle against the Burmese are all on display. There is even a life-sized model of a war elephant. Whether it is Buddha statues of all sizes, hardwood furniture with lavish mother-of-pearl inlays, exquisite jewellery, coins or valuable porcelain – Thailand's entire cultural wealth, its religion and history are splendidly displayed in this museum. Also worth a look at is *Wat Buddhaisawan*, built in 1795 with its magnificent murals and Buddha statues. The temple is located right at the front entrance of the museum. *Wed–Sun 9am–4pm, free tours in English Thu 9.30am | admission fee 200 baht | Na Phra That Rd (am Sanam*

Siam's treasures: encounter the nation's fabled past in the National Museum

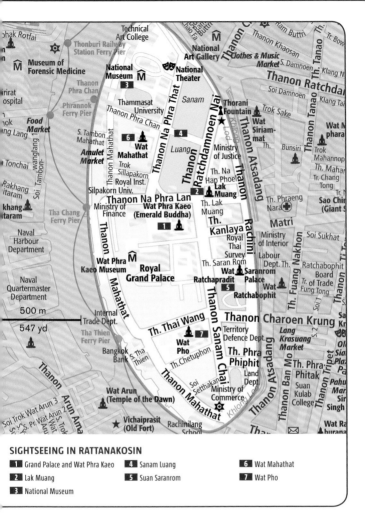

SIGHTSEEING IN RATTANAKOSIN

1 Grand Palace and Wat Phra Kaeo   **4** Sanam Luang   **6** Wat Mahathat

2 Lak Muang   **5** Suan Saranrom   **7** Wat Pho

3 National Museum

---

*Luang) | www.thailandmuseum.com, www.
museumvolunteersbkk.net*

4 SANAM LUANG
(120 B4–5) *(𝄞 B3)*
The open space in front of the Grand Palace
that is fringed with blooming, flaming red
tamarind trees is more than an just an

oval field. It is the place of kings. This is
where royalty were cremated in public
ceremonies. But joyful occasions also take
place here, so every year in May a royal
ploughing ceremony takes place to mark
the beginning of the rice-growing season.
Farmers travel from all over the country
and swarm onto the field to gather some

of the symbolically sown rice grains in order to mix them with their own grain for luck. From February through April, when the winds are favourable, the skies over Sanam Luang are splashed with colourful kites in the late afternoons. Kite flying has a long tradition in Thailand and they even host international kite competitions. And if there is nothing going on when you are there then you can simply rest on a bench and contemplate the Grand Palace or have your palm read by one of the local fortune-tellers. *Ratchadamnoen Nai Rd*

⑤ SUAN SARANROM 120 B6) *(🗺 B4)*
What is today a park was once the royal garden and formed part of *Saranrom Palace*. The park is open to all, but the palace remains closed to tourists as it houses the Foreign Ministry. Even though it is located near the Grand Palace, this small oasis is only visited by only a handful of tourists. *Daily 9am–9pm | Sanam Chai Rd*

⑥ WAT MAHATHAT
(120 A5) *(🗺 B3)*
This royal monastery with over 100 Buddha statues, houses the Buddhist *Mahachu-* *lalongkorn University*. Not only for Thais, meditation courses for foreigners are also offered here *(daily 7–10am, 1–4pm and*

RELAX & ENJOY

The ● *Health Land* in the city offers various wellness oases. Even at the entrance of the wonderfully decorated spas you get a sense complete harmony. And with an aroma therapy massage or a milk bath in the jacuzzi you will be in seventh heaven. *Health Land* measures up to the top hotels, but is considerably cheaper. A two-hour long traditional Thai massage, for example, only costs 440 baht. Not even the many massage shops that you find at every street corner in Bangkok are cheaper. Of course you can find the more expensive places but here you will feel like royalty with the four-hour long *Royal Thai Package* for 9600 baht. *Daily 9am–11pm | on Srinkakarin, Sathorn, Pinklao, Ekkamai, Chaeng Wattana and Asok Street | www.healthlandspa.com*

The soles of the reclining Buddha in Wat Pho are decorated with mother-of-pearl inlays

6–8pm) at the *International Buddhist Meditation Centre (www.mcu.ac.th/IBMC/ html/course.html).* Participation is free of charge, but a donation is welcome. There is a large market held here every Sunday that sells traditional medicines, antiques, amulets and Buddha figures. *Daily 9am– 5pm | free admission | Na Phra That Rd (at the Thammasat University)*

🟥 WAT PHO ⭐
(120 B6) (*m* B4)

South of the Grand Palace is Wat Pho, the monastery of the reclining Buddha, which is even older than the city itself as it was already in existence in the 16th century. It was rebuilt in 1781, a year before the actual formation of the city, and it was renovated over a period of 17 years in the 19th century. Wat Pho remains the most extensive monastery complex in Bangkok. The main attraction is the 45m/148ft long and 15m/49ft high golden Buddha. His reclining position symbolises Buddha's transition into a state of nirvana.

The monastery is a mandatory stop on every city tour. The massive onslaught of people and the press of souvenir sellers are not exactly condusive for a meditative mood. Nonetheless, Wat Pho is definitely worth a visit. One reason is the ● Thai massages that are offered here: the massage school of the monastery is the most famous in the entire country. INSIDER TIP The best times for a massage are in the mornings or late afternoons, when the demand is not so high. A one-hour foot massage costs 360 baht, a herbal mas-

Foot massage at Wat Pho

sary)| point of entry at Chethuphon Rd | www.watpho.com | express boat: Tha Tien

BANGLAM-PHOO

Those who travel around Thailand with a backpack will in all likelihood come to this district at Chao Phraya and not only because it is in the immediate vicinity of the Grand Palace.

Nowhere else in Bangkok will you find as much cheap accommodation packed in to as tight a space as here. Banglamphoo is Asia's backpacker stronghold and is globally unique. Even if you don't stay here, you should visit and have a look at how international backpackers have changed entire streets where once there were only Thais. But not all of them have made their homes into guest houses or shops with tourist knick-knacks. If you stroll up the alleys where there are no English advertisements, you will experience the charm of the old Banglamphoo, a district of traders and artisans. You will discover small street markets and streets filled with temple monasteries where you can catch your breath. *MRT: Hua Lampong/Skytrain: National Stadium, from there about 20 minutes each by taxi | Saen Saep khlong boat: Tha Phanfa (at the Golden Mount, from there 10 minutes on foot) | Chao Phraya express boats: Tha Phra Athit, Tha Wat Sam Praya, Tha Wisut Kasat*

sage 480 baht *(daily 8am–5pm | www.watpomassage.com)*. The traditional massage is a remnant of the centuries old medical tradition of the monastery: Wat Pho was a famous healing site for the sick until the 1970s.

Warning: there are always touts lurking about between Wat Pho and the Grand Palace who tell visitors who are unacquainted with the area that the temple or the palace is closed for a Buddhist holiday. They then try to lure you to fly-by-night business so that they can sell you fake goods. *Daily 8am–5pm | admission fee 50 baht (temple tours cost 200 baht, for two people 300 baht, but is not neces-*

■1 DEMOCRACY MONUMENT
(120 C4) (*ʃʃ* C3)

In 1932 Thailand's absolute monarchy was abolished after a peaceful coup and was replaced by a constitutional democracy. This monument, in the midst of the traffic, symbolises the democratic rebirth of the nation. It is not aesthetically pleasing, but

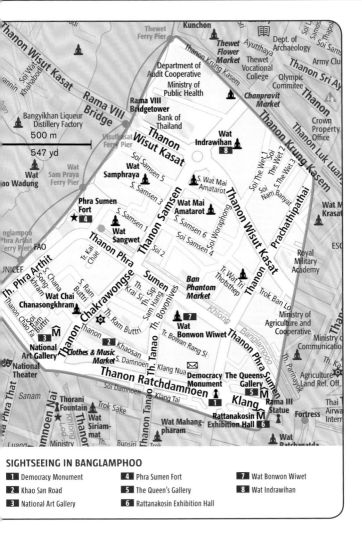

SIGHTSEEING IN BANGLAMPHOO

1. Democracy Monument
2. Khao San Road
3. National Art Gallery
4. Phra Sumen Fort
5. The Queen's Gallery
6. Rattanakosin Exhibition Hall
7. Wat Bonwon Wiwet
8. Wat Indrawihan

it is of great importance to the Thais. Whenever there are coup attempts by the military, the city's pro-democracy supporters rally here. And in May 1992 some protestors who stood up for democracy at the Democracy Monument even lost their lives here. *Ratchadamnoen Klang Rd*

2 KHAO SAN ROAD ★
(120 B–C4) (*ω C2*)

During the hippie era it was Chicken Street in Kabul or Freak Street in Kathmandu, today is it Bangkok's Khao San Road: a street with a cult status in the backpacker scene. It all started back in the 1980s with a few simple guest houses that have now mushroomed into dozens and many have been revamped into small hotels, some of them even have swimming pools. The street is about 400m long and it is geared towards backpackers with accommodation, Internet cafés and bars and pubs that offer muesli and spaghetti alongside fried rice. There are tattoo shops for skin art and nose, tongue and belly piercings while hawkers and shops sell jungle boots and silver jewellery and pirated copies of the latest hits. Everything a backpacker may need can be bought in this one stretch.

The Khao San Road is a pedestrian zone in the evenings when it becomes a loud and colourful food alley, bazaar and an open air party. Thais also enjoy coming here to see the crazy *falang*, the pale-skinned foreigners. It is a bit quieter in the side streets. And you will feel right at home in the **INSIDER TIP** backpacker district at the Monastery Chanasongkhram near the river. www.khaosanroad.com

3 NATIONAL ART GALLERY ●
(120 B4) (*ω B2*)

Contemporary art and antique works by Thai artists can be viewed at the National Art Gallery. The exhibition includes some paintings by the monarch King Bhumibol as well as art works from different epochs –

The Khao San Road: a 400m long backpacker's dream

the colonial building itself is worth a visit. *Wed–Sun 9am–4pm | admission fee 30 baht | Chao Fa Rd (north of the National Museum) | www.thailandmuseum.com*

4 PHRA SUMEN FORT
(120 B3) (*🗺 B2*)

The fort was built in 1783, a year after the city was founded. The hexagonal construction, which is armed with canons, is one of the original 14 watchtowers along the old city wall. This fort together with the Phra Sumen Fort and the Mahakan Fort at the Golden Mount, are the only ones that have not been torn down. The whitewashed building can only be viewed from outside. The fort is surrounded by a small, pleasant park that is the ideal place to relax and to pass the time. *Daily 5am–10pm | Phra Athit Rd | express boat: Tha Phra Athit*

5 INSIDER TIP THE QUEEN'S GALLERY
(121 D4) (*🗺 D3*)

This gallery, which is under royal patronage, exhibits works by Thai artists and has a wealth of paintings, sculptures and installations on five floors. Contemporary as well as traditional works are on display. Even though The Queen's Gallery is only a short walking distance from the backpacker district, only a few tourists find their way here. *Thu–Tue 10am–7pm | admission fee 30 baht | 101 Ratchadamnoen Klang Rd (next to Bangkok Bank) | www.queengallery.org | Saen Saep khlong boat: Tha Phanfa (3 minutes on foot from there)*

6 INSIDER TIP RATTANAKOSIN EXHIBITION HALL
(121 D5) (*🗺 D3*)

A bird's eye view of the Grand Palace: this interactive museum has an exact model of Bangkok's most famous building. It is just one of the many exhibits that present the history, art and culture of Bangkok's oldest city district, Rattanakosin. A multimedia show gives insights into the year 1782, when Bangkok was founded. The museum, which is equipped with the latest technology, provides an impressive overview of the glamour of bygone eras. And from the observation deck in the fourth floor you can see the old city live. Sights like the Golden Mount and the iron temple, Wat Ratnada (Loha Prasat), seem to be an arm's length away. *Tue–Fri 11am–8pm, Sat/Sun 10am–8pm | admission fee 200 baht | 100 Ratchadamnoen Klang Rd | at the Wat Ratnada | www.nitasrattanakosin.com | Saen Saep khlong boat: Tha Phanfa | 5 minutes on foot from there*

Buddha in the Wat Indrawihan

tor doing an operation. The temple has a special meaning for the Thais because Prince Mongkut was an abbot here before he took to the throne as Rama IV. The current monarch, King Bhumibol, spent two weeks in this monastery as a monk in 1956. *Daily 9am–6pm | free admission | Phra Sumen Rd | near Khao San Rd | Saen Saep khlong boat: Tha Phanfa*

8 INSIDERTIP WAT INDRAWIHAN
(121 D2) (*D1*)

Worshippers place lotus flowers at the feet of the monastery's 32m/105ft high Buddha. It is believed that there is a relic of The Enlightened One in the head of the statue. Very few tourists visit this temple monastery in the north of Banglamphoo. *No fixed opening hours | free admission | Wisut Kasat Rd*

CHINATOWN & PAHURAT

⭐ **In Chinatown business takes place around the clock. Whether it is oranges or material, tools or washing machines – you can find almost everything here. And all that glitters might actually be gold.** Yaowarat Road in Chinatown is the centre for the Thai trade in jewellery, most of which is made of almost pure gold. The attraction of this area lies in its alleys and side streets. Every house, whether modern or old and weathered, is also a shop or restaurant, Business is done on the ground floor and families live upstairs. Pavements, when they exist, are storage facilities and trading place.

Pahurat is the Indian version of Chinatown, a district that could be Bombay. The district is full of Hindus and Sikhs who usually sell fabrics. There are also countless numbers of Indian tailors who live here

7 INSIDERTIP WAT BONWON WIWET ● (120 C4) (*C2*)

This monastery is a green oasis with ponds full of fish and turtles. It is worth seeing for its murals with subjects that you do not expect to see in a temple; horse races, European-style buildings and even a doc-

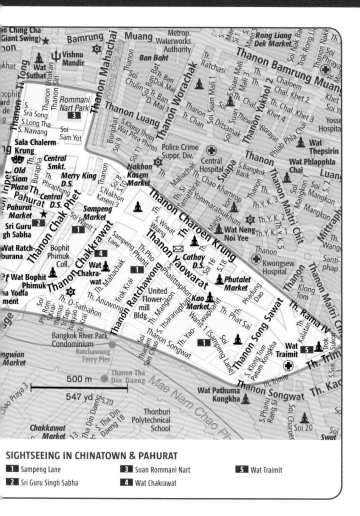

SIGHTSEEING IN CHINATOWN & PAHURAT

1 Sampeng Lane **3** Suan Rommani Nart **5** Wat Traimit

2 Sri Guru Singh Sabha **4** Wat Chakrawat

---

in and even independent textile dealers fly in from India to look for bargains in Bangkok's Little India. Of course there is also everything else that belongs to the Indian way of life; hot spices, sweet perfumes and the latest Bollywood videos. In small pubs you can tuck into freshly baked *chapati* (flat bread) and a plate of *dhal* (lentils). *MRT: Hua Lampong, 10 minutes on foot from there to Chinatown (10 minutes by taxi to Pahurat) | Chao Phraya express boat: Tha Ratchawong, Tha Saphan Phut*

1 INSIDER TIP SAMPENG LANE
(126 A–B2) (*∅ D5*)

This narrow alley (in Thai: Soi Wanit) in Chinatown is where the old Bangkok still thrives. Many of the crowded shops look the same as they did a hundred years ago. There are pharmacies with highly polished wooden counters, dimly-lit corner shops and a lots of fabric shops. The Sampeng Lane is not a tourist shopping street but it is fascinating to browse through. Only for those who are comfortable with crowds.

◪ SRI GURU SINGH SABHA
(125 E1) (*∅ C4*)

This is the second largest Sikh temple outside of India, and it apparently cost 100 million baht to build. Its elegantly simple marble temple and golden dome does seem to reflect the price. By contrast, the interior design with shops that fit snugly under the dome, paints a rather more functional and austere picture. *Daily 8am–6.30pm | free admission | Chakpetch Rd | in Pahurat (Little India) | entrance in a small street next to the shopping centre India Emporium*

◪ SUAN ROMMANI NART
(120–121 C–D6) (*∅ C–D4*)

If you feel a little hemmed in this park, it is with good reason: the watchtowers on the park's borders were once part of a prison. In 1992 it was torn down except for the towers and two smaller buildings (*today the Prison Museum | Mon–Fri 8.30am–4pm | free admission*) and transformed into a green oasis with jogging path. This is a good place to take a break on your way from the Grand Palace to Chinatown. *Daily 5am–9pm | corner Charoen Krung/Maha Chai Rd*

◪ INSIDER TIP WAT CHAKRAWAT
(126 A2) (*∅ D5*)

The only monastery in Thailand – and perhaps the world – where you get to see crocodiles. Three of these well-nourished reptiles live in a pool. However, Thais do not come here for the crocodiles, but to pray in front of Buddha's shadow in a grotto here. *Daily 8am–6pm | free admission | Chakrawat Rd (between Chinatown and Pahurat)*

◪ WAT TRAIMIT
(126 C2) (*∅ E5*)

This monastery near the main railway station houses a colossal treasure: 3m/10ft high Buddha weighing 5.5 tons that is approximately 700 year old. It is made of pure gold – at least according to the official version. Where did the Thai people manage to acquire such an enormous amount of gold when they founded their first kingdom? After all, no significant amounts of gold have ever been found in South East Asia. For a long time no one even knew about the existence of this figure, because the golden Buddha was hidden under a coat of plaster – possibly to safeguard it from Burmese invaders. It was only in 1955 that the plaster cracked to reveal the remarkable golden Buddha. In 2010 a museum was opened in the monastery which tells the story of the Buddha. The story of Chinatown is told in the division *Yaowarat Heritage Centre* through miniatures, life-sized figures, photos and many exhibits. *Viewing of the Buddha daily 9am–5pm, museum closed on Mondays | admission fee to the Buddha 40 baht, to the museum 100 baht | Trimit Rd*

SILOM & LUMPHINI PARK

Silom Road with its many banks and office towers, shops and hotels is one of the busiest streets of the city. At

Just join in: yoga in Lumphini Park

lunchtime bankers and office workers in ties and suits flock to the mobile fast food stalls.

In some of the side alleys you can still find the traditional Bangkok, with weathered shop-houses and old city villas set in green gardens. The main tourist magnet is the side alley, Patpong for its bars. As the Suan Lum Night Bazaar at the Lumphini Park was torn down in 2011, Patpong is now the only remaining tourist night market in the inner city. East of Silom Road the traffic noise dies down and you can hear birds twittering. In Lumphini Park wide green lawns under shady trees offer lots of space for a nap. *MRT: Lumphini, Silom | Skytrain: Sala Daeng, Chong Nonsi*

▮▮ LUMPHINI PARK ★ ● ☺
(128 B–C 3–4) (*Ⓜ J–K 6–7*)

The largest and best known park in the inner city is Bangkok's green lung. While the traffic piles up outside, paddle boats float on the man-made lake, lovers stroll hand in hand, families picnic, stressed city workers snooze in the shade of old trees, and at dawn early risers start their day with t'ai chi and yoga. At the open air fitness centre muscle men lift weights while couples practise their dance steps in the pavilion. There is plenty going on here but you will always find a quiet spot somewhere. And if you discover on your stroll through the park one of its 2m/6.6ft long tongue-flicking dragons, don't fret. They are harmless monitors that eat fish from the park lake or search for chicken bones and other leftover food that visitors leave behind after their picnic. Kites in the sky are also a sight to behold: when the wind is right (between February and April) it is not only children that fly their kites here. Musical highlights are the free Sunday afternoon concerts by the Bangkok Symphony Orchestra *(www.bangkoksym phony.org/concertinpark.html)* in December, January and February. At the park entrances mobile dealers sell snacks and drinks. *Daily 5am–8pm | points of entry: Rama IV Rd, Ratchadamri Rd, Sarasin Rd, Witthayu Rd*

Colourful pantheon:
the Sri Mariamman Temple

■ PATPONG (128 A4) *(ⓜ H7)*

As notorious as Hamburg's Reeperbahn, Patpong is the city's red light and entertainment area. It covers two parallel side streets full of clubs, restaurants, go-go bars and stalls selling tourist souvenirs and knick-knacks. These stands have become a tourist attraction known as *Patpong Night Bazaar* and the area is popular with Thai families in the evenings. In recent years a number of bars have closed down and reopened as a souvenir shop. *Between Silom and Surawong Rd*

■ SILOM ROAD (127 D–F5, 128 A–B 4–5) *(ⓜ F–J 7–8)*

This is also known as Bangkok's Wall Street. The stock exchange is situated elsewhere, but many of the city's banks are located here. For tourists this street is one of the most popular shopping miles. At lunchtime it is full of office workers who eat at the many fast food stalls. And in the evening hawkers display their goods on the pavements, especially in the upper part of the road at the Skytrain station Sala Daeng. The street name comes from the windmills *(silom)* that once brought canal water to the surrounding fields. A sculpture serves as a reminder of this time that is long since past.

■ SNAKE FARM (127 F3–4) *(ⓜ H6)*

There are 180 species of snakes in Thailand, 56 of them have are deadly. At the Snake Farm you can watch employees of the Queen Saowapha Memorial Institute milk venomous snakes like the king cobra. The farm, founded in 1923, is the second oldest in the world. Even though it attracts many visitors, the Snake Farm is not primarily a tourist attraction, but rather a research institute and laboratory where antiserum is produced to help victims of snake bites. *Mon–Fri 8.30am–4.30pm, Sat/Sun 8.30am–noon, venom extraction*

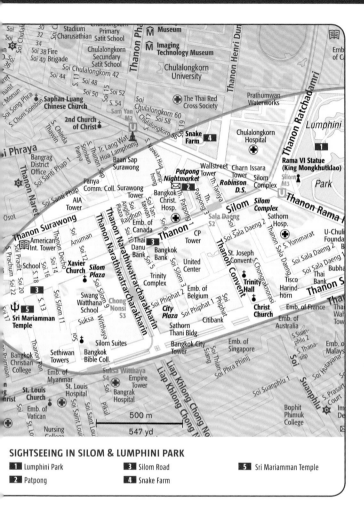

SIGHTSEEING IN SILOM & LUMPHINI PARK

1 Lumphini Park　　　**3** Silom Road　　　**5** Sri Mariamman Temple

2 Patpong　　　　　**4** Snake Farm

Mon–Fri 10.30am and 2pm, at the weekend only 10.30am | admission fee 70 baht | corner Henri Dunant/Rama IV Rd (across from Lumphini Park)

5 SRI MARIAMMAN TEMPLE

(127 D5) (*𝄝 G7*)

All of India's gods adorn this Hindu temple and its brightly coloured statues make it a popular photo opportunity. If you ask a Thai about the Sri Mariamman, he will probably not be able to help you but when you say *Wat Khaek* it will ring a bell – because this is what the locals call this colourful temple. *Khaek* is Thai for people from the subcontinent: from India, Pakistan and Bangladesh. *No fixed opening times | free admission | Silom Rd/corner Pan Rd*

PRATHUNAM/ SIAM SQUARE/ SUKHUMVIT

A word of warning: if you are afraid of the urge to splurge then you should steer clear of this area.

At first glance everything here seems to be geared towards commerce. Gigantic shopping malls, mega stores, a huge market maze and hoards of street vendors await customers. Bangkok's glittering shopping world is concentrated around the Skytrain station Siam Central where there is one shopping centre after another, the biggest being Siam Paragon. The other side of the street, with its maze of shops around Siam Square, attracts the city's fashion-conscious youth from nearby Chulalongkorn University.

Further up over Ploenchit Road to Sukhumvit Road there is a permanent shopping frenzy which even extends to the pavements – especially the lower Sukhumvit Road – which are covered with stalls. Many tourists come here, because nowhere else in Bangkok can you find as many hotels crammed into such a small area.

The market district, Prathunam, gives you another impression. Here you will also find a labyrinth of shops and stalls, but mostly for Thais that are shopping for cheap clothing. But not everything in this area has to do with shopping. You will also find plenty of places of interest which are worth interrupting your shopping spree for. *MRT: Sukhumvit | Skytrain: Phaya Thai, National Stadium, Siam Central, Chit Lom, Ploen Chit, Nana, Asok | Saen Saep khlong boat: Tha Jim Thompson, Tha Prathunam, Tha Wit-thayu, Tha Nana*

SIGHTSEEING IN PRATHUNAM/SIAM SQUARE/SUKHUMVIT

■ BAIYOKE SKY HOTEL ✻
(123 E5) (*ℳ J3*)

A highlight in Bangkok: this hotel reaches 309m/1013ft into the sky. For visitors there is an observation deck with windows on the 77th floor. On the 84th floor an open air skywalk rotates 360 degrees. On clear days, which are unfortunately rare, you can see the Gulf of Thailand. *Daily 10.30am–10.30pm | admission fee 120 baht | Sky*

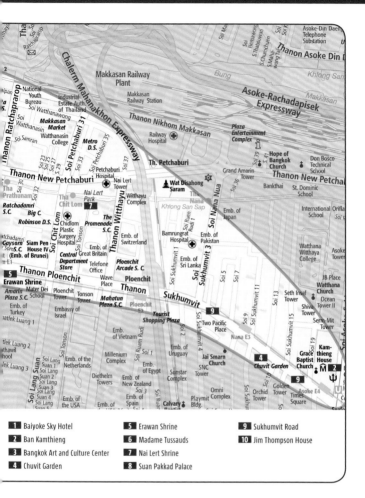

1 Baiyoke Sky Hotel
2 Ban Kamthieng
3 Bangkok Art and Culture Center
4 Chuvit Garden
5 Erawan Shrine
6 Madame Tussauds
7 Nai Lert Shrine
8 Suan Pakkad Palace
9 Sukhumvit Road
10 Jim Thompson House

Restaurant guests (buffet 11am–2pm and 6pm–10pm | Moderate) on the 76th and 78th floor are allowed on the platforms free of charge | 222 Ratchaphrarop Rd (at the Prathunam Market)

2 BAN KAMTHIENG
(129 F2) (*M5*)

A *ban* is a house or a village. The *Siam Society* is based in these old teak houses from northern Thailand that are over 160 years old. On display are fishing and farming tools – nothing spectacular but if you are staying on Sukhumvit Road anyway, it is just around the corner. The Siam Society organises presentations and excursions all over the country. *Tue–Sat 9am–5pm | admission fee 100 baht | 131 Soi Asoke (side street 21 left off Sukhumvit Rd) | www.siam-society.org*

3 **INSIDER TIP** **BANGKOK ART AND CULTURE CENTER** ●
(122 C6) (*H4*)

Art, sculpture or music, film, photography or theatre: this art centre is where all the aspects of contemporary art and design come together. The avant-garde of the Thai art scene is represented here with exhibits of their works. But there are also exhibits of foreign artists as well. In an area of 32,500ft² various art forms are shown in temporary exhibitions that each last a few weeks. Individual exhibitions give artists the stage for the different presentations. This museum is a must for those interested in Thailand's contemporary art scene, the building itself is a work of art with its clean and modern architecture. *Tue–Sun 10am–9pm | free admission (individual exhibitions additional charge) | 939 Rama I Rd (direct access from the Skytrain station National Stadium) | www.bacc.or.th*

4 **CHUVIT GARDEN** ●
(129 E2) (*M5*)

Chuvit Garden is a small, very well maintained green oasis with strict rules (no cigarettes, no walking on grass) right at the hubbub of Sukhumvit Road. The park is named after Chuvit Kamolvisit, who made a fortune from massage parlours. Until 2003 there were more than 100 illegal stalls with bars and shops occupying the land. During a night raid these stalls were flattened. Chuvit was taken to court but was not found guilty of the raid. He then created this park for the general public (on land that is worth millions) but he did so with the knowledge that you cannot take your riches with you when you die. At dusk the lanterns cast a glow that gives the whole area a peaceful and meditative atmosphere. *Daily 6am–10pm and 4–8pm | free admission | Sukhumvit Rd/Corner Soi 10*

5 **ERAWAN SHRINE** (128 B–C1) (*J4*)
This shrine is dedicated to the Hindu god Brahma. Actually it is a larger than life spirit house. When the Erawan Hotel (now the Grand Hyatt Erawan) was built in the 1950s, there were a number of fatal accidents. The shrine was built to pacify the spirits of the site. From that moment on-

KEEP FIT!

So, do you feel like springing into action? Then jump on a mountain bike and ride out into nature! Why not go to where the farmers paddle to their vegetable fields and where there are wooden stilt houses, where the thick vegetation and temple ruins wait to be discovered. Some of the areas around the outskirts of Bangkok city are almost as they were a hundred years ago. The tour guides from *Grasshopper Adventures* take riders in groups of up to eight people out to these areas on their *Tour Bangkok Countryside* trip. In case you start to have doubts as to whether or not you are truly still near the million-strong metropolis, just look out to all the high-rise buildings in the distance. The day trip including lunch costs 1600 baht. Book at least one day ahead of time. *Tue, Thu, Sun, also for groups of four people daily | Grasshopper Adventures Shop | 57 Ratchadamnoen Rd (near Khao San Rd) | tel. 0 22 80 08 32 and 0 87 929 52 08 | www.grasshopperadventures.com*

Offerings of flowers and candles: divine intervention at the Erawan Shrine

wards, no more workers died and the shrine became famous throughout the country. Barmaids and bankers alike come to ask for divine intervention and young women in splendid costumes will perform ritual dances for a small donation. The Brahma statue that you can see here today is however, a copy. The gold plated original was destroyed by a mentally ill man in 2006. The attack cost him his life – locals chased him and beat him to death only a few metres away from the shrine. *Corner Ploenchit Rd/Ratchadamri Rd*

▇ **6** MADAME TUSSAUDS ●
(127 F1) (Ⓜ H4)

The wax museum has opened its tenth branch in one of the most stylish shopping centres in Bangkok. If you have ever wanted to sit next to US President Obama in the Oval Office or be photographed with Brad Pitt and Madonna, now is your opportunity. A total of 70 celebrities are on display, standing or sitting as though

they were real. About 20 of them are famous only in Thailand though. The current king is obviously not one of the wax figures but his parents are on their thrones in the splendid *Royal Room*. These two figures are the only ones that are not allowed to be touched. *Daily 10am–9pm | admission fee 800 baht | Siam Discovery Centre, 6th floor | Rama I Rd | www.madametussauds.com/bangkok*

▇ **7** INSIDER TIP ➤ NAI LERT SHRINE
(123 F6) (Ⓜ K4)

The private Nai Lert Park is the garden of the Swissôtel Nai Lert Park Bangkok is a green oasis with splashing fountains and waterways. In one corner (freely accessible but fenced off from the hotel garden) near the car park are hundreds of wooden and stone phalluses. The collection is dedicated to the goddess of fertility Chao Mae Tabtim and is not that easy to find. Do not go through the hotel (the management frowns upon it) but walk from

Ploenchit Road up Soi Chitlom and turn right shortly before the bridge over the Saen Saep canal into Soi Somkit. After a few minutes you will find the car park, the shrine is on your left-hand side. *Swissôtel Nai Lert Park Bangkok | 2 Witthayu Rd*

■8 SUAN PAKKAD PALACE
(123 D4) (*Ш J3*)

Five traditional Thai houses set in a tropical garden make up this palace, once the residence of Princess Chumphon. Her passion was collecting art and antiques. You can marvel at ivory carvings, jewellery, porcelain, furniture and many more handcrafts. One of the buildings (the pavilion) is itself a work of art with its richly lacquered interior walls. *Mon–Sat 9am– 4pm | admission fee 100 baht | Sri Ayudhaya Rd (north-west of the Baiyoke Sky Hotel) | www.suanpakkad.com*

■9 SUKHUMVIT ROAD
(129 E–F 2–3) (*Ш L–M5*)

This street seems to go on forever. And as a matter of fact it only ends after 430km (267mi), shortly before the Cambodian border. Its name stays the same for its entire length. For tourists the most interesting section is the area between the side streets Soi 1 and Soi 24 where there is a profusion of hotels, restaurants, department stores, shopping centres, wholesalers and shops. Every few metres there are also travel agents, tailors and Internet cafés. There are also many pubs and go-go bars waiting for clientele. In the late afternoons fast food stalls and hawkers open up for business along the pavements. The start of Sukhumvit Road is Bangkok's most important tourist centre.

■10 JIM THOMPSON HOUSE ★ ●
(122 B6) (*Ш G4*)

Born in America in 1906, Jim Thompson rebuilt Thai silk production after World War II. This made him a living legend in the kingdom but he was also shrouded in mystery as he was reputed to be connected to the CIA. Thompson disappeared without a trace in the mountains of Malaysia in 1967. When you enter his house today, you get the feeling that he has only just left. And you will understand why his residence, completed in 1959, was the talk of the town and a meeting point of high society. The 'house' consists of six different teak structures in the traditional Thai style with high roofs and pointed gables. Every single building is a treasure chest: Thompson was a passionate collector of Asian artefacts and antiques and collected sculptures, porcelain, paintings and much more. The most

valuable items in his collection are the Buddha statues from the 7th century as well as the French maps of Siam from the 17th century. Tour guides explain all there is to see. *Mon–Sat 9am–5pm | admission fee 100 baht | Soi Kasemsan 2, Rama I Rd | www.jimthompsonhouse.com*

IN OTHER DISTRICTS

Besides the tourist districts you can discover many places of interests, some of which – like the Golden Mount – can be done together with a visit to the historic old city.

It is definitely worthwhile to get off the tourist track because away from the crowds you will find that Bangkok is indeed a city with many different faces. And that contrary to popular belief, there are in fact many places that are not crowded. You need to venture away from the shopping mile Sukhumvit Road or the backpacker centre around Khao San Road.

ANCIENT CITY (130 C3) (*ᗕ 0*)

The entire country is an open air museum: even the outlines of the 370 acres of park were measured according to Thailand's actual borders. There are 116 significant attractions in the Ancient City (in Thai: *Muang Boran*) in miniature format or to a 1:1 scale. The most beautiful palaces,

The whole of Thailand in a beautiful park: famous structures in the Ancient City

A mountain for Buddha: the chedi on the Golden Mount conceals a relic

temples, monuments and ruins are rebuilt in finest detail. And a canal was specifically emptied for the floating market. *Daily 8am–5pm | admission fee 350 baht (tram ticket additional 100 baht, bicycle hire 50 baht). The park is situated 33km/20.5mi on the Sukhumvit Rd south-east of Bangkok in Samut Prakan province. You can book organised tours in any hotel or travel agent | tel. 0 27 09 16 44 | www.ancientcity.com*

INSIDER TIP ► BENJAKITI PARK ● ☺
(129 F3–5) (*ወ M6–7*)

This well-looked after parkland on an ½mi long lake is the best kept secret in the entire city. Even though the park is near the busy Sukhumvit Road and is even next to an underground station, it is an oasis of calm. There are neither souvenir shops nor food stalls to attract tourists en masse. Visitors can use the paddle boats or canoes on the lake and rent bicycles for a cycle around the lake to get some exercise. There is also a Buddha statue and an *International Garden* with a variety of tree species planted by foreign diplomats. The lake is lined with colourful bougainvillea bushes. Early in the morning or evening joggers do their rounds. During the day you practically have the park all to yourself. There is a promenade along the banks of the lake. The park is on the grounds of the huge state-owned Thailand Tobacco Monopoly. For years there has been talk of moving the cigarette manufacturing to the provinces and making the entire 80ha area into a park. But to date most of the manufacturing buildings still stand. *Daily 5am–9pm | Ratchadapisek Rd | MRT: Queen Sirikit Convention Centre*

GOLDEN MOUNT 🎋
(121 D5) (*ወ D3*)

The *Phukao Thong* (Golden Mountain) is an 80m/262ft high, artificial hill at the Wat Saket. The golden tower *(chedi)* houses a Buddha relic. A further climb up 318 steps and Bangkok lies at your feet. The monastery at the foot of the mountain is one of the oldest in the city. *Daily 7.30am–5.30pm | admission fee 10 baht | Boripat Rd | Saen Saep khlong boat: Tha Phanfa*

INSIDER TIP ▶ PEDESTRIAN HIGHWAY ☺
(129 D–F3) (*𝄞 K–M6*)

In the middle of the metropolis is a road without stalls, potholes and scooters and very few pedestrians because even the locals have never heard of this mile-long nameless road. It is actually a highway for pedestrians (in part elevated a few metres above ground) and leads from *Ratchadapisek Road* (Benjakiti Park) to *Witthayu Road* (Lumphini Park). The first part follows a canal, where monitor lizards swim, passing by old wooden houses, banana trees and coconut palms. Afterwards the path passes through a very traditional suburb and almost over the roofs of houses. Steps lead over the *Mahanokhon Expressway* and the Witthaya Road, which is just 100m from Lumphini Park.

There is no signage and it is not easy to find. Turn from Sukhumvit Road at the Skytrain station Asok to the right into Ratchadapisek Road (direction Benjakiti Park). After about 100m right after a footbridge a few narrow metal steps on the right lead down to the canal. It looks pretty unkempt here, but at the end of the staircase there is a fence with a thoroughfare which leads into a cul-de-sac, lined with wooden houses and a few small shops. After about 300m on the right hand side is a wooden bridge (the entrance is controlled by the government-owned tobacco manufacturer) that crosses the canal. Directly before the bridge on the left hand side is a concrete path. Follow this path to the last steps at the end. Then take the steps on the left and a turn right into Witthayu Road to Lumphini Park.

Entrance to this path is also possible from *Sukhumvit Road*. Go to *Soi 10* until the end, where a gate blocks the way over a makeshift bridge to the tobacco manufacturers. The gatekeeper will let you climb over without a problem. The pedestrian highway starts immediately to your right after the bridge.

KING PRAJADHIPOK MUSEUM ●
(121 D5) (*𝄞 D3*)

This museum, which is not often visited, is dedicated to the country's last absolute monarch – King Prajadhipok – who had to step down in 1932 and was exiled to England. Exhibits, photos and writings detail the life of the unhappy monarch and also a particularly radical era in Thailand's

LOW BUDGET

▶ Ferry boats commute the whole day between Bangkok and Thonburi and will take you to Chao Phraya's other river bank for just 3 baht, for example to *Wat Arun (p. 54)*.

▶ The *One Day Pass* for the Skytrain and Mass Rapid Transit only costs 120 baht each. The ticket is valid all day and allows you to avoid all the traffic.

▶ You can travel back and forth on the Chao Phraya with the *Chao Phraya Tourist Boat* for 150 baht with the *One Day River Pass* (tickets available at the Skytrain stations Nana and Siam as well as Saphan Taksin and directly at Sathorn Pier).

▶ Free admission to all the less popular monasteries, for example *Wat Mahathat (p. 32)*.

Exquisite barge carvings in the Royal Barge Museum

history. *Tue–Sun 9am–4pm | free admission | 2 Lan Luang Rd (near Golden Mount) | www.kingprajadhipokmuseum.org*

ROYAL BARGE MUSEUM
(120 A3) (𝖬 A2)

The Royal Barge Museum is one of the obligatory stops on the khlong tours in Thonburi. Visitors get to see eight of the most beautiful of 50 barges. They are artistic and decorated with mythical creatures and are still rowed today at royal ceremonies on the Chao Phraya. On the water they are far more impressive than when displayed in the storage halls. Flagship of the fleet is the 45m/146ft long Suphannahong barge (Golden Swan). *Daily 9am–5pm | admission fee 100 baht | at the confluence of the Bangkok Noi canal into Chao Phraya | www.thailandmuseum.com | express boat: Tha Phra Chan*

SAO CHING CHA (120 C5) (𝖬 C3)

This giant swing was built in 1784, two years after the city was founded, on the orders

of Rama I. Up until 1935 courageous men risked their lives to earn a bag of coins by swinging 25m/82ft high. Those who succeeded only received three tamlung (worth twelve baht today) and as so many people lost their lives trying, the competitions were finally prohibited. Today a replica of the Sao Ching Cha (without the swing) stands at the Wat Suthat in the middle of the Bamrung Muang Road. *MRT: Hua Lampong, then 15 minutes by taxi*

THAILAND CREATIVE & DESIGN CENTER ● (0) (𝖬 0)

Design encompasses everything that has form, whether clothing, flower arrangements or bathroom tiles. Thai artists display their designs here with temporary exhibitions. This creative centre, supported by the government, contributes towards making Bangkok a design metropolis. The works of foreign designers are also on display. There is a permanent exhibition of Italian Vespas and American

Barbie dolls. There is also a library of 25,000 (mostly English) books about art, architecture and design along with a souvenir shop and a 🥄 café with a gorgeous view of the city. The TCDC is situated in the upmarket Emporium shopping centre and is a favourite meeting place for creative young Thais. *Tue–Sun 10.30am–9pm | free admission | on the 6th floor of the Emporium shopping centre | Sukhumvit Rd, Soi 24 | www.tcdc.or.th | Skytrain: Phrom Pong (direct entry)*

THONBURI ★ ●

(124–125 A–F 1–6) (*Ø A–E 1–8*)
Thonburi, at the western embankment of the Chao Phraya, is a part of Bangkok and older than the metropolis itself. Thonburi was a small city when Bangkok was still a village called Ban Makok and served as the port of entry for the former capital, Ayutthaya. After Ayutthaya was destroyed by the Burmese in 1767 the capital was moved to Thonburi. But 15 years later Rama I founded the capital anew on the other side of the river.

Although there are still traffic jams on Thonburi's main streets, canals *(khlongs)* create a spider web of waterways, which divides this part of the city into a mosaic of islands. When you take a boat cruise, you will understand why early travellers to Bangkok called it the 'Venice of the East'. You can book organised tours at any travel agent. But the large tour boats are not able to navigate the small canals – where Thonburi comes across as remarkably rural with shingle-covered wooden stilt houses – so it is a better option to rent a motor boat and helmsman and INSIDER TIP explore the water labyrinth on your own. But you will have to make it clear to the captain beforehand that you do not want to go where everyone else is. You can rent a boat at every pier but your chances of finding a helmsman who understands English are better at the piers at the Skytrain station Saphan Taksin *(Tha Sathorn)*, the Grand Palace *(Tha Chang)*, the River City shopping complex *(Tha River City)* and at the Oriental Hotel *(Tha Oriental)*. Count on 600 to 700 baht

Follow the canals: a wide network of waterways branch out across Thonburi

an hour. Negotiating is mandatory! Do not let boat pilots guide you to the piers as you will have to pay them a commission. And try not to fall for the 'free tour'. They usually take you to dubious shops that sell fake jewellery.

VIMANMEK ROYAL PALACE
(121 E1) (*ω 0*)

The largest teak palace in the world – King Chulalongkorn resided here around 1900. It contains a wealth of old photos, antiques, paintings, jewellery and gifts of state in 31 exhibition rooms. Warning: visitors wearing shorts or miniskirts will not be allowed in. *Daily 9.30am–3.15pm | traditional Thai dances at 10.30am and 2pm | admission fee 100 baht (dropped if you bring with your ticket from the Grand Palace) | Ratchawithi Rd (at the Dusit Zoo) | www.palaces.thai.net | Skytrain: Victory Monument, then 15 minutes by taxi*

WAT ARUN ★ (124 C1) (*ω B4–5*)

The 'temple of the dawn' at Chao Phraya on the Thonburi side is a city, with its 79m (about 260ft) high *prang*, a tower richly decorated with porcelain and colourful glass. Steps lead up to ⚓ observation decks. Even if the highest is closed, you will still have an amazing view over Bangkok. The *prang* is outlined against the setting sun in a filigree silhouette on the horizon. *Khlong* tours also stop at Wat Arun. From Pier Tha Tian behind Wat Pho, ferries cross over from 6am–10pm to Pier Tha Arun. *Daily 8am–4pm | admission fee 50 baht | Arun Amarin Rd | www.watarun.org*

WAT BENJAMABORPIT ★
(121 F2) (*ω E1*)

This jewel of a temple is made out of Italian Carrara marble and is a must on every city sightseeing tour. Dazzling white, it stands in a park, guarded by two marble lions and surrounded by 52 Buddha statues. The roofs of the temple, covered with red tiles, are staggered in cascades and have golden tips at their gables. There is also a canal (with three little bridges) that is full of turtles that were released by the faithful as offerings. *Daily 9am–5pm | admission fee 20 baht | Sri Ayutthaya Rd | www.watbencha.com | Skytrain: Victory Monument, then 15 minutes by taxi*

WAT RATCHABOPIT
(120 C6) (*ω C4*)

This temple is not part of the usual sightseeing tours and that is exactly why it is

THAI BOXING

Thai boxing or *Muay Thai* is considered to be the most difficult martial art in the world. Blows with fists and elbows, kicking with your feet and kneeing are all allowed. But Thailand's national sport is not just a wild brawl in the ring, but an ancient tradition, bound in ceremonial rules. Every fight starts out with the boxer doing a ritualistic dance and invocation. In Bangkok the country's best boxers get into the ring in the *Ratchadamnoen Stadium (Mon and Wed 6pm, Thu 5pm and 11pm, Sun 4pm and 8pm | admission fee 500–2000 baht | Ratchadamnoen Nok Avenue near Khao San Rd)* and also the *Lumpini Boxing Stadium (Tue and Fri 6.30pm, Sat 3.30pm and 8pm | admission fee 1000–2000 baht | Rama IV Rd at Lumphini Park | www.muaythailumpini.com).*

Buddhist novices enjoy the magnificent view of the temple Wat Arun

worth a visit. There are no souvenir sellers and no food stalls to distract you from its high *chedi* – the pointed tower – and walls that are decorated with painted tiles and golden reliefs. The temple doors with their mother-of-pearl inlays are also exquisite. *Daily 5am–6pm | free admission | corner Atsadang/Ratchabopit Rd (in the centre of the historic city) | MRT: Hua Lampong, then 10 minutes by taxi*

INSIDER TIP WAT RATNADA
(121 D5) (*M D3*)
Many Buddhist temples resemble each other, but this temple's construction is unique. It is 35m/115ft high and built like a three-tiered pyramid. 37 slim, spiral towers surround the temple which symbolise the 37 wise sayings of Buddha. The towers are made of iron, which is why the Thais call it *Loha Prasat*: Iron Palace. It is the only remaining temple construction in this style in the world, it was modelled on one in Sri Lanka. There is a daily market at the monastery where amulets and Buddha statues are sold. *Daily 9am–8pm | free admission | Mahachai Rd (at the Golden Mount) | Saen Saep khlong boat: Tha Phanfa*

WAT SUTHAT (120 C5) (*M C3*)
The temple, centrally situated in the old city, is famous for its exquisite murals, which were restored at considerable expense; they tell the stories of 28 Buddha followers. The ordination hall is also remarkable and it is considered to be the most beautiful in Thailand. Rama I laid the foundation stone of this monastery, which counts as one of the most significant of the land. It houses a 14th century bronze Buddha statue which came from Sukhothai, the first Thai capital. In front of the temple you can see the giant swing *Sao Ching Cha*. Many shops of the shops around the temple sell religious items. *Daily 9am–5pm | free admission | Bamrung Muang Rd | MRT: Hua Lampong, then 10 minutes by taxi*

FOOD & DRINK

In Bangkok you will be tempted with food everywhere you go, because Thais delight in eating. There is always something sizzling or simmering on every corner at any time of the day. The mobile fast food stalls are just as a part of the cityscape as are the traffic jams.

On hissing gas cookers, over charcoal fires and in woks the mobile chefs grill and steam delicious snacks and light meals in a flash – from soup through to rice to seafood.

Culinary highlights need not be expensive as many top restaurants offer lunch specials. Even in Bangkok's most expensive gourmet temple, *Le Normandie* in the Oriental Hotel, you can get a set lunch menu (without drinks) for about 1200 baht. All the better restaurants have a service charge of 10 or 7 per cent VAT. If you want to go out for dinner, it is best to make a reservation. Tip: restaurant reviews are found at *www.dininginthailand. com* and at *www.asiatatlerdining.com/ thailand* you can search for restaurants according to price and location. Most restaurants in Bangkok are open throughout the day, usually 11am–10pm, however, many top restaurants only offer lunch (11.30am–2pm) and dinner (6pm–10pm). Thai cuisine is not only delicious but also fiendishly hot. Where lots of foreigners

Photo: Vertigo restaurant

Hot, exotic and healthy: in Bangkok you can eat like a king as every street corner offers food that is fresh, cheap and delicious

dine, the cooks go easy on the chilli. To be safe you should say *mai peht* (not hot) when you place your order. There are always little bowls of chilli on the restaurant tables. There are ones with chopped dried chillies and sugar (the locals like to add this to their noodle soup), with fresh chillies (in a sweet-and-sour vinegar sauce) and ones with a light brown sauce. The latter is called *nam pla* and is a fish sauce

that is used as a salt substitute, when mixed with chopped chillies it becomes firewater, *pik nam pla*.

Thai cuisine is considered to be one of the healthiest in the world. It contains very little fat and lots of vitamins and plenty of fresh ingredients. Everything is also prepared quickly which means that the vegetables stay crisp. Rice is their staple diet and the Thai word for eating *(kin kao)* translates as 'to consume rice'. The unique Thai taste comes from a myriad of herbs and spices: coriander, lemongrass, ginger, basil, tamarind – and naturally garlic and chilli. Meat is used sparingly and it is usually chicken. Fish and seafood, on the other hand, are served often.

The meals are served bite-sized and you

The nobles could afford to let the eyes feast as well: their dishes were arranged like works of art. The top restaurants still celebrate this tradition, for example *Celadon* in the Hotel Sukhothai and *Salathip* in the Shangri-La. The capital's gourmet chefs are keen to experiment and there are also many foreign chefs in the top restaurants

The fresh ingredients in Thai cuisine are thanks to the numerous food markets in Bangkok

eat with a spoon, and the fork is used to place the food on the spoon but chopsticks are used for noodle dishes (and soups). Usually a Thai menu consists of various dishes that are placed on the table along with a big pot of rice. You take a large portion of rice and then small portions of the individual dishes.

A special highlight is the Royal Thai Cuisine. It originated in the palace kitchen and dates back to the kingdom of Ayutthaya.

creating 'fusion' food by mixing Thai recipes with the cuisine of other countries. A very popular combination is the fusion of Mediterranean and Thai cuisine which works well because it is light and also uses a lot of seafood.

THAI DISHES

Thai cuisine has been strongly influenced by the Chinese, one classic example is that early immigrants from the ancient

China brought with them noodles. A typical breakfast that shows its origin through its name is *kanom chin*, cold rice noodles with an extremely hot curry sauce as well as fresh herbs and pickled vegetables. You will have the taste of neighbouring Malaysia with sweetish curry dishes like the *gaeng massaman*. The papaya salad *som tam* originated in Laos, but this is not something you find in restaurants but rather at markets and on street stalls. The Thai love their food hot but even their beloved chilli is an import – Portuguese seamen once brought some with them from Brazil. Thailand's most well known dish is *tom yam*, a slightly sour and hot soup, spiced with lemongrass, coriander, ginger and tamarind. When you add crab it becomes *tom yam gung* and with fish it becomes *tom yam pla*. Also delicious: *Kao niau mamuang*, sticky rice and mango, sweetened with coconut milk, it is an excellent snack and is also sold at all the markets and on street stalls.

DRINKS

You can buy any of the well known brands of soft drinks on every street corner. Even the shops that don't stock groceries often have a fridge for soft drinks. However, the choice of fresh fruit juices is limited to orange juice which in smaller restaurants is sometimes mixed with lemonade. The best option for fruit and vegetable juice is at the drinks stalls at the Skytrain stations, for example in Siam Central and Phrom Pong. There are all sorts of beers available, local as well as imported. Two Thai favourites are *Chang* and *Singha*. More expensive beers are *Tiger* and *Heineken*, also brewed in the country under licence. According to law, alcohol may only be sold in shops from 11am to 2pm as well as from 5pm to midnight. Corner shops are not that strict with these restrictions. Thailand's favourite spirit is *saeng som*, distilled rum made from sugar cane, which is also considered a 'whiskey'. The locals like to drink it on ice with soda water and a dash of lemon juice. In the tourists bars this is the standard drink, but it usually gets mixed with Coca-Cola.

FRUIT

The cheapest fruits are bananas, pineapple, papaya and watermelon. But try the other fine fruits to be found in the tropics. The markets are full of the kinds of goodies that you can only find in delicatessens back home. For many Thais the durian is the king of fruits. It looks like a large spiked medieval mace and its smell will knock you out. The taste of the creamy fruit flesh is a blend of vanilla and cheese, and you will either be addicted to it, or you

Rough outside, tasty inside: the flesh of the rambutan tastes sweet and aromatic

will hate it. Everyone will like the mangosteen *(mangkut)*. Its wine-red skin hides a juicy, white fruit flesh that tastes sweet and sour simultaneously. You should also not miss out on the hairy rambutan *(ngo)*, the noble litchi *(lin chi)* and the red Java apples *(chom pu kio)*.

CAFÉS & BISTROS

INSIDER TIP ▶ BANGKOK BAKING COMPANY (129 E2) *(𝄞 L5)*
Great selection of croissants, baguettes, cakes and salads at the Hotel Marriott's bistro. Air-conditioned or in the open air. *Daily 6am–11pm | 4 Sukhumvit Rd | Skytrain: Nana, Ploen Chit*

INSIDER TIP ▶ DASA BOOK CAFÉ (0) *(𝄞 0)*
Espresso, caffè latte, pastries, second-hand books and friendly people make this little bookshop-cum-café something special.

Daily 10am–8pm | 710/4 Sukhumvit Rd | between Soi 26 and 28 | www.dasabook cafe.com | Skytrain: Phrom Phong

LANDMARK CAFÉ (129 E2) *(𝄞 L5)*
Delicious tarts, pralines and light snacks in the open air in front of the Landmark Hotel. *Daily 10am–10pm | 138 Sukhumvit Rd | Skytrain: Nana*

DINNER CRUISES

You can book dinner tours on the Chao Phraya in any tourist office. There are numerous tour operators like *Thai River Cruises (www.thairivercruises.com), Chaophraya Cruises (www.chaophrayacruise. com)* and *Loy Nava (www.loynava.com)*. Many top hotels in Bangkok have their own boats that cruise to and fro on the river. Cheaper and shorter than dinner tours are sunset cruises (drinks only) at sundown.

APSARA ★ ● (126 C4) (*∅ E7*)

This teak barge is a floating gourmet restaurant. Royal Thai Cuisine is served on deck and is prepared by chefs from the luxury hotel Banyan Tree that also owns the boat. A romantic dinner option. *Departure Fri/Sat 7.45pm from River City Pier | set menu 2375 baht | tel. 0 26 79 12 00 | www.banyantree.com*

HORIZON (126 C6) (*∅ E8*)

Modern river cruise with air-conditioning and open deck. Opulent buffet with Thai and international delicacies. The Hotel Shangri-La is the owner, which speaks volumes in terms of quality. *Departure daily 6.30pm from the hotel pier Tha Shangri La | buffet 2300 baht | tel. 0 22 36 77 77 | www.shangri-la.com/bangkok | Skytrain: Saphan Taksin*

FAST FOOD STALLS

Pavement cooks are practically everywhere. Some have stationary mini kitchens at a regular location (and also with regular customers), while others wheel their mobile stoves to where the action is and to where many people gather. In certain city streets these stalls are particularly numerous.

CHINATOWN: Especially fans of noodle dishes and Chinese specialties, like toast with sweet chilli sauce, will be spoilt for choice here. As dusk approaches *Yaowarat Road* (126 A–B 1–2) (*∅ D–E5*) thousands of pots steam and sizzle and the cooking and grilling continues until the early hours of the morning.

SILOM ROAD/CONVENT ROAD: In this district of banks and businesses, the pavements change drastically at lunchtime into open air restaurants. You will find one fast food stall after another in the eastern part

Silom Road (towards Lumphini Park) and its side street, Convent Road (128 A4–5) (*∅ H7*). The second time the hungry crowds visit this street is at two in the morning, when Patpong's bars close. Skytrain: Sala Daeng

SUKHUMVIT ROAD: In the lower part of Sukhumvit, in the side street Soi 3 to Soi 19 (129 E–F2) (*∅ L–M5*) the street vendors and cooks take turns on the pavements. When the vendors take down their stands at around 11pm, the kitchens come rolling in and wait for the night owls who stream out of the bar districts Nana Plaza and Soi Cowboy. Many of the side streets also have food stalls during the day. *Skytrain: Nana* In the ● Soi 38 off Sukhumvit Road (0) (*∅ 0*) the pavement food stalls really get going after midnight. In this prestigious residential area (Thonglo) with its fine clubs and restaurants the pavement gastronomy also presents itself with great

LOW BUDGET

▶ Affordable gourmet cuisine: the restaurants in the city's top hotels all compete for custom and many offer excellent value for money lunch menus. For as little as 400 baht you can dine in high-class restaurants. See the 'Bangkok Post' for all the special offers.

▶ Massive choice at minimum prices: the large shopping centres all offer a huge selection of meals. Thai, Chinese, Indian, and Mediterranean – everything is there. Best options are: *Siam Paragon, Central World, Emporium, Mah Boonkrong (all on the Skytrain route).*

finesse with options like fried noodles and grilled squid on the menu, but night owls with deeper pockets prefer the freshly grilled langoustines, king prawns or fish in chilli sauce. *Skytrain: Thong Lo*

RESTAURANTS: EXPENSIVE

INSIDER TIP ▶ BOUCHOT (0) (*⋒ 0*)

Oysters, prawns and fish – this chic restaurant specialises in seafood. The seafood is either local or imported from France. Absolutely delicious: mussels in white wine sauce. Eat like royalty in Bangkok, outstanding value for money. *Daily | Sukhumvit Rd, Soi 24 (Oakwood Residence) | tel. 0 22 58 55 10 | www.bouchot-restaurant. com | Skytrain: Phrom Pong*

THE DOME ★ ☼
(127 D5) (*⋒ F8*)

If you want to be in heaven in this lifetime, this is the right address. At 220m/720ft on the roof of Hotel Lebua you will have to decide between a number of options. There is the air-conditioned *Mezzaluna* that serves the finest Italian cuisine. The spectacular glass suspension bridge to

GOURMET RESTAURANTS

Biscotti (126 B2) (*⋒ J5*)
There are a lot of Italian restaurants in Bangkok but this restaurant is a jewel that serves delicacies like tuna tartar or seafood risotto with artichokes. *Daily | dinner menu from 1200 baht | Four Seasons Hotel | 155 Ratchadamri Rd | tel. 0 21 26 88 66 | www.fourseasons. com/bangkok | Skytrain: Ratchadamri*

Celadon (128 C5) (*⋒ J7*)
The finest of the restaurants that serve Royal Thai cuisine. For real treat try the charcoal-grilled river shrimp or the banana blossom salad. There is also wide selection of vegetarian dishes on offer. *Daily | dinner menu from 1400 baht | Sukhothai Hotel 13/3 | Satorn Tai Rd. | tel. 0 23 44 88 88 | MRT: Lumphini, then 5 minutes by taxi*

The China House (126 C5) (*⋒ E8*)
Whether it is the bird's nest soup or the marinated squid with 'hundred-year' duck eggs: you will not find better Chinese (Cantonese) cuisine anywhere else in Bangkok. *Daily | dinner menu from 1400 baht | Hotel Oriental 48 | Oriental Avenue | tel. 0 26 59 90 00 | Skytrain: Saphan Taksin*

Le Normandie (126 C5) (*⋒ E8*)
Many consider this to be the finest French restaurant outside of France. With a bit of luck you may get a window table with a panoramic view. The wine list is extensive and the evening dress code is strictly black tie. Book at least a day in advance. *Daily | dinner menu from 3600 baht | Hotel Oriental 48 | Oriental Avenue | tel. 0 26 59 90 00 | Skytrain: Saphan Taksin*

Salathip (126 C6) (*⋒ E8*)
Royal Thai cuisine is celebrated in three teak pavilions by the river in the garden of the Hotel Shangri-La. The dishes are all very artistically arranged. *Daily | dinner menu from 1200 baht | Shangri-La Hotel 89 | Soi Charoen Krung 42/1 | tel. 0 22 36 77 77 | Skytrain: Saphan Taksin*

the seafood restaurant *Breeze* or Martinis in the *Distil Bar*. The best option for a romantic evening or a champagne cocktail is however the highest open air restaurant in the world: the *Sirocco* (Western Mediterranean cuisine) with its ● *Sky Bar* on the 63rd floor. Cocktails simply taste heavenly up here. *Daily | State Tower | 1055 Silom Rd | tel. 0 26 24 95 55 | www.lebua.com | Skytrain: Surasak*

FACE ★ (0) (𝄞 0)

Three themed restaurants at one address: the *Hazara* serves the best North Indian cuisine in an exotic ambience; *Lan Na Thai* has the charm of ancient Siam (both lunch and evenings). A real visual and culinary highlight. Or if you prefer sushi the *Musaki* (evening only) offers Japanese delicacies. Lots of locals eat here and tourists are a rare sight. *Daily | lunch 11.30am–2.30pm, dinner 6–10.45pm | 29 Sukhumvit Rd, Soi 38 | tel. 0 27 13 60 48 | www.facebars.com | Skytrain: Thong Lo*

SPICE MARKET
(128 B2) (𝄞 J5)

In the style of an old spice shop, this restaurant is one of the best Thai restaurants in the city. For a real treat try the prawn with asparagus or the red curry with duck. *Daily | Four Seasons Hotel | 155 Ratchadamri Rd | tel. 0 21 26 88 66 | www.fourseasons.com/bangkok | Skytrain: Ratchadamri*

VERTIGO ✤
(128 B5) (𝄞 J7)

Not quite as high as the Sirocco. But the grilled fish, accompanied by jazz music in the open air 200m/656ft above the city is just as much of a highlight. Your sundowner cocktail will be mixed for you at Moon Bar next door. *Daily | Hotel Banyan Tree | Satorn Tai Rd | tel. 0 26 79 12 00 | www.banyantree.com | MRT: Lumphini*

For the best Chinese cuisine: China House

RESTAURANTS: MODERATE

BAAN KHANITHA (0) (𝄞 0)

In a wonderful old building, the finest Thai chicken such as chicken with lemongrass or fish in a banana leaf is served on teak tables. *Daily | 36/1 Sukhumvit Rd, Soi 23 | tel. 0 22 58 41 81 | www.baan-khanitha.com | Skytrain: Phrom Phong*

LOCAL SPECIALITIES

▶ **gaeng kiau wan gai** – a delicious green curry with chicken and aubergines that will make you sweat, even though it is slightly sweet *(wan)*. Served with rice.

▶ **gaeng massaman** – a red curry with beef strips, peanuts and potatoes (quite hot)

▶ **gung hom pa** – a crispy delicacy of shrimp in batter with tartar sauce or sweet-and-sour sauce with chilli

▶ **kao pat** – or fried rice, this is always a substantial meal. Prepared with egg *(kai)* and vegetables *(pak)* and also crab *(gung)*, chicken *(gai)* or pork *(mu)*

▶ **kui tiao nam** – this noodle soup is Thailand's favourite in-betweener and it is served at every fast food stalls. Mostly with pork or chicken but especially tasty with duck *(pet)*

▶ **pla piau wan** – sweet-and-sour fish is also a visual feast as the sauce is prepared with colourful vegetables and pineapple pieces (photo on right)

▶ **plamuk tohd katiam pik thai** – squid strips, fried with garlic and pepper

▶ **som tam** – salad made with thin strips of unripe papaya with cocktail tomatoes, dried shrimp, peanuts and lots of chilli. Best with raw vegetables, sticky rice and grilled chicken *(gai pat)* (photo on left)

▶ **tom kha gai** – a chicken and coconut milk soup that is a particularly exotic delight. Warning: you will also find whole chillies in the broth

▶ **tom yam gung** – this spicy sour shrimp soup is Thailand's unofficial national dish. Lemongrass gives it its taste and chilli its spiciness. Best with rice.

BEI OTTO (129 F3) (*M6*)

Otto Duffner has long been an institution in Bangkok. When German celebrities are in the city and are in the mood for some good German home cooking, then they come here for the potato salad or roast pork. Duffner makes his own sausage and bakes bread, rolls and pretzels (also sold on the street). *Daily | Sukhumvit Rd, Soi 20 | tel. 0 22 62 08 92 | www.beiotto.com | Skytrain: Asok, Phrom Phong*

LE DALAT INDOCHINE ★
(0) (*0*)

Its interior is French colonial but the cuisine is authentically Vietnamese, just like the kind of food enjoyed in a Vietnamese home. Of course spring rolls are served, but also fish with vegetables and fresh herbs. *Daily | 14 Sukhumvit Rd, Soi 23 | tel. 0 26 61 79 67 | Skytrain: Asok | MRT: Sukhumvit*

INSIDER TIP ▶ EAT ME
(128 A5) (*ΦΦ H7*)

The interior design is minimalist and the meals creative: like their tuna tartar with parsley root salad. The most expensive thing in this chic restaurant are the pictures on the walls. *Daily | Convent Rd, Soi Pipat 2 | tel. 0 22 38 09 31 | www.eatme restaurant.com | Skytrain: Sala Daeng | MRT: Silom*

ERAWAN TEA ROOM
(128 B1) (*ΦΦ J4*)

Not only does this elegantly nostalgic restaurant in the Erawan Shopping Centre serve the largest selection of teas in Bangkok but they also serves classic Thai cuisine from curry through to *pad thai* (fried noodles). It is managed by the neighbouring hotel Grand Hyatt Erawan.

Daily | 494 Ploenchit Rd | tel. 0 22 54 12 34 | Skytrain: Chit Lom

INSIDER TIP ▶ HARMONIQUE
(126 C5) (*ΦΦ F7*)

Charming little restaurant, filled with antiques. Sit at traditional tea house tables and enjoy best the Thai-Chinese home cooking like their large black mushrooms filled with crab meat, or cucumber salad with shrimp. *Closed on Sundays | 22 Charoen Krung Rd, Soi 34 | near the Surawong Rd junction | tel. 0 26 30 62 70 | express boat: Tha Wat Muang Khae*

RANG MAHAL ★ ☆ (129 F3) (*ΦΦ M6*)

Their classic North Indian cuisine is not only heavenly because it is served high up on the 26th floor of the Hotel Rembrandt. Try the lamb marinated in herbs overnight or order a mixed starter platter worthy of a maharajah. Make sure you reserve a table at the window, and then you will have the city at your feet. *Daily | Rembrandt Hotel | 19 Sukhumvit Rd, Soi 18 | tel. 0 22 61 71 00 | Skytrain: Asok | MRT: Sukhumvit*

Delicious meals served on traditional tea house tables at Harmonique

INSIDER TIP ▶ **TAPAS CAFE**
(129 E2) (*M5*)

You are quite right if you think this sounds Spanish to you. Tapas are the latest trend in Bangkok and this is the restaurant that started it all. Now there are quite a few

framed condoms on the wall. The restaurant is run by a birth control and AIDS prevention organisation and everyone receives a condom with the bill. The food is excellent, they serve Thai food that has just the right level of spiciness for the

Front row seat at the river: The Deck with its view of Wat Arun in Thonburi

restaurants that offer tapas, for example Sunday Brunch. But the original is still where you get the most delicious tapas outside of Barcelona. *Daily | Sukhumvit Rd, Soi 11 | in a hidden little side street Suk 11, branch of Soi 11 after the Zanzibar restaurant | tel. 0 26 51 29 47 | www.tapasia restaurants.com | Skytrain: Nana*

RESTAURANTS: BUDGET

CABBAGES & CONDOMS
(129 F3) (*M5*)

Cabbages and condoms? Don't be put off by the name of this restaurant nor the

Western palate. You can also dine outside in the tropical garden. *Daily | 10 Sukhumvit Rd, Soi 12 | tel. 0 22 29 46 10 | www.pda. or.th/restaurant | Skytrain: Nana | MRT: Sukhumvit*

CENTRAL FOOD LOFT ★
(128 C1) (*K4*)

Top class fast food at low prices on the 7th floor of the Central Chitlom shopping mall: you can try a variety of international cuisines and even combine them. Why not try some sushi as a starter and lasagne as a main course? Whether Thai, Chinese, Vietnamese, Japanese or Italian: everything is freshly prepared in front of you. *Daily | Central Chitlom Department Store | Ploenchit Rd | Skytrain: Chit Lom (direct entrance)*

INSIDER TIP CHILLI CULTURE (129 E1) (*M4*)

An enormous variety of authentic Thai dishes but you must remember to specify how hot or how mild you would like your dish. Whether beef salad or lotus root with pork mince – the meals served here are so delicious that even the locals are impressed. *Daily | Sukhumvit Rd, Soi 11 (at the end of the road) | tel. 0 22 54 28 82 | Skytrain: Nana*

CRÊPES & CO (129 F3) (*M6*)

Philippe Brutin's imagination has no limits when it comes to the fillings for his French crêpes. His *Crêpe Sukhumvit* with chicken, onions, tomatoes, garlic, coriander and béchamel sauce is delectable. Also savoury dishes from Morocco, Greece, Spain, Bulgaria and a selection of drinks that range from Moroccan peppermint tea to French cider. *Daily | 18/1 Sukhumvit Rd, Soi 12 | tel. 0 26 53 39 90 | www.crepes.co.th | Skytrain: Asok | MRT: Sukhumvit*

INSIDER TIP THE DECK (125 D1) (*B4*)

Hidden at the end of a small street behind the Wat Pho is this jewel of a restaurant on the river. Squid or mushroom risotto eaten outside on the deck with a view of the 'temple of the dawn' Wat Arun is the best. *Daily | Hotel Arun Residence | Soi Pratu Nokyung | tel. 0 22 21 91 58 | www.arunresidence.com | express boat: Tha Tien*

HIMALAYAN KITCHEN (120 C4) (*C2*)

A whiff of Nepal welcomes you to this Indian restaurant: Nepalese vendors enjoy dining here and the cheap price of their dhal and chapati also makes it very popular with the backpackers in the area.

Daily | 1 Khao San Rd | tel. 0 26 29 22 71 | Saen Saep khlong boat: Tha Phanfa

KUPPA (129 F3) (*M6*)

With its massive glass front and the unique interior made from metal, cement and rattan it is and eye catching sight. International dishes ranging from grilled fish with mashed potatoes, to pizza to Thai cuisine. It includes a coffee roasting section. *Closed Mondays | 39 Sukhumvit Rd, Soi 16 | tel. 0 26 63 04 95 | Skytrain: Asok | MRT: Sukhumvit*

ONCE UPON A TIME (123 D5) (*J3*)

The Frenchman Pierre Delalande is the owner of this restaurant in an old wooden house full of historic photos that give it a museum-like atmosphere. Authentic Thai cuisine. *Daily | 32 Petchaburi Rd, Soi 17 (near Amari Watergate Hotel) | tel. 0 22 52 86 29 | www.onceuponatimeinthailand.com | Saen Saep khlong boat: Tha Prathunam*

THE STABLE (129 E2) (*L5*)

North European snacks: this restaurant serves the widest selection of Danish sandwiches in Bangkok. There is also the option to sit outside on the terrace. There is a barbeque at the pool in the hotel garden every evening. *Daily | The Stable Hotel | 39 Sukhumvit Rd, Soi 8 | tel. 0 26 53 00 17 | www.stablelodge.com | Skytrain: Nana | MRT: Sukhumvit*

INSIDER TIP YONG LEE RESTAURANT (129 F2) (*M5*)

The tables are almost falling apart, space is tight, and you can hear the noise of the traffic outside. And yet this restaurant is always full. This is because there is no where cheaper serving such great Thai-Chinese cuisine in the area. *Daily | Sukhumvit Rd / corner Soi 15 | Skytrain: Asok | MRT: Sukhumvit*

SHOPPING

CITY **WHERE TO START?**
The entire city is one shopping area with no clear boundaries between residential and business districts. The best shopping options are between the two Skytrain stations of Chit Lom and Siam Central which is linked by the pedestrian bridge, the **Skywalk (128 A–C1)** (*🗺 H–J4*) that runse beneath the elevated train train route. Two exclusive shopping centres, the Siam Paragon and Central World, are a must.

You should travel to Bangkok with empty suitcases. Because you will need lots of packing space for the return trip! Anyone who leaves this city without excess baggage would have to be someone who loathes to shop. Thailand's capital is a shopper's paradise.

In the gigantic shopping centres, countless retail stores and at vibrant weekly markets you will be spoilt for choice. Not to mention the armies of mobile pavement vendors, who convert streets into shopping miles. And everything is much cheaper than back home. This applies not only to the classic Thailand gift ideas like textiles, leather goods or crafts. You will be able

This is the city for bargain hunters so be prepared to rise to the occasion – Bangkok is all about shopping and wild spending sprees

to get international fashion and accessories, glasses, spices, medication, digital cameras, computers and even cutlery in Bangkok at prices which are often far more reasonable than those at home.

Bargaining is mandatory almost everywhere the only exception is department stores and supermarkets where you can not bargain – but they constantly have items on special. At retail stores a discount is almost always included. Rule of thumb: start your bargaining at about 50 per cent below that of the dealer's price and agree to about two thirds of the original price. To get a feeling for acceptable prices, you should first get three or four prices from different dealers before you decide on your purchase. This is especially important at the markets and with the street vendors in the tourist areas.

Computer, software, cameras: get them all at the Pantip Plaza

By the way: you shouldn't haggle for the last baht. From a Thai perspective, someone who bargains down too strongly (when he can afford more) is not doing their moral duty to help those who are not as economically advantaged as they are. Department stores, shopping centres and stores are open from 10am until 9pm (many until 10pm) on a daily basis. Most of the street vendors offer their goods from the afternoon until late at night. Going shopping in tropical Bangkok can be quite stressful due to the large distances but it need not be: you can use the air-conditioned Skytrain or the MRT which will take you to all the important shopping areas in record time.

ANTIQUES

There are antiques on every corner but of course not everything that looks old is as it seems and there is an entire industry that makes knock-offs and copies in Thailand. According to estimates up to 80 per cent of the available 'antiques' are counterfeit. So buying antiques in Bangkok is something best left to the experts and there is also the added issue of getting the correct authorisation to take pieces out of the country. The same applies to reproductions. You will need a professional to assist in getting the correct export authorisation and if you decide to organise the official papers on your own you must take into account a waiting period of about two weeks. *Information available at the Department of Fine Arts | Naphratad Rd at the National Museum | tel. 0 22 21 48 17 and 0 22 21 78 11*

INSIDER TIP THE COLONIAL LEGEND
(129 D2) *(Ø K5)*
Exquisite collection of antiques, handicrafts and affordable household items from colonial times. *20/21 | Soi Ruam Ruedi (side street from Ploenchit Rd) | tel. 0 22 55 53 54 | Skytrain: Ploen Chit*

RIVER CITY SHOPPING COMPLEX
(126 C4) (*ⓜ E6–7*)

Bangkok's largest shopping centre for antiques and arts and crafts with about 100 shops selling items primarily from China and South East Asia. Auctions on the first Saturday of the month at 1.30pm. There is an exquisite selection of historical land maps on the 4th floor at INSIDER TIP *Old Maps & Prints* (www.classicmaps.com). *Yotha Rd (at the Hotel Royal Orchid Sheraton) | tel. 0 22 37 00 77 | www.rivercity.co.th | express boat: Tha River City*

SILOM GALLERY (127 D5) (*ⓜ G7*)

Almost all the shops distributed over its four floors sell antiques and handicrafts and you can buy beautiful models of old sailing ships on the third floor at *The Fine Arts. 19 Silom Rd (at the Hotel Holiday Inn) | Skytrain: Surasak*

BUDDHA STATUES

They are everywhere – in antique shops for many thousands of baht or at street vendors and in souvenir shops at reasonable prices. However is it officially forbidden for non-Buddhists to export these statues without the proper authorisation. The exportation of historically valuable Buddhas is generally not allowed. A proper dealer will make you aware of this and will organise official authorization for you. Generally speaking there are no strict controls at airport departures but should you get caught with a Buddha statue, especially a valuable one, you can be sure that it will be confiscated and you will also have to pay a considerable fine.

BOOKS

ASIA BOOKS

Largest book shop chain with a huge selection of books in English and other languages. *Branches: Central World (Ratchadamri Rd) | www.asiabooks.co.th | Skytrain: Chit Lom* (123 E6) (*ⓜ J4*) *| Landmark Hotel (Sukhumvit Rd) | Skytrain: Nana* (129 E2) (*ⓜ L5*) *| Times Square (Sukhumvit Rd) | Skytrain: Asok | MRT: Sukhumvit* (129 F2) (*ⓜ M5*)

COMPUTERS & CAMERAS

PANTIP PLAZA
(123 D5) (*ⓜ J3*)

Bangkok's largest department store for computers and cameras has 320 branches. Software is very reasonable here but the Pantip also happens to be the centre of software piracy and even regular raids by the authorities have not been able to

---

⭐ **Central World**
Lots of shopping and snacking → p. 72

⭐ **Siam Paragon**
Exclusive shopping paradise → p. 73

⭐ **Central Chitlom**
Ideal for the ultimate shopping spree → p. 74

⭐ **Narai Phand**
Thailand's largest selection of crafts → p. 76

⭐ **Chatuchak Weekend Market**
Purported to be the largest flea market in the world → p. 76

⭐ **Siam Paradise Night Bazaar**
Plenty of stalls for a nighttime shopping spree, also has a large beer garden → p. 78

MARCO POLO HIGHLIGHTS

make a difference. *Phetburi Rd (near Prathunam Market) | Saen Saep khlong boat: Tha Prathunam*

SHOPPING CENTRES

CENTRAL WORLD ★ ●
(128 B1) (*m J4*)

An enormous complex of 500 shops and over 100 cafés and restaurants makes this the biggest lifestyle shopping complex in South East Asia. Everything is exclusive and it is light and spacious, so that even large crowds are easily accommodated and it regularly hosts fashion shows and exhibitions. There is a cinema and a giant supermarket on the top floor. *Ratchadamri Rd | www.centralworld.co.th | Skytrain: Chit Lom (direct access)*

EMPORIUM
(0) (*m 0*)

Over 180 shops and dozens of restaurants, delicatessens and confectionary stalls on six floors, including a department store. You can find practically everything here from the finest crockery to mobile phones, also many famous jewellers, watchmakers and boutiques selling top international brands. For those with a sweet tooth, make your way to the ● patisserie division on the top floor where there is a large selection of baked confectionary, chocolate, pralines and tarts. **INSIDER TIP** *It's happened to be a closet (itshappened tobeacloset.wordpress.com)* on the second floor has an eccentric name and unique service – the shop is a combination of boutique and bistro. Here you will find Bangkok's funkiest and most colourful fashions and accessories for women. For a delicious gourmet experience, there are treats like salmon carpaccio or duck breast in plum sauce. *Sukhumvit Rd (at Soi 24) | www.emporiumthailand.com | Skytrain: Phrom Phong (direct access)*

ERAWAN
(128 B1) (*m J4*)

Elegant setting, with fine shops that offer mostly jewellery, watches and clothing. You will also find a wellness centre and the Erawan Tea Room here. *Ploenchit Rd (at the Erawan shrine) | Skytrain: Chit Lom (direct access)*

GAYSORN PLAZA
(128 C1) (*m J4*)

Exclusive boutiques and foreign luxury brands and a wide selection of restaurants. *Ploenchit Rd/corner Ratchadamri Rd | www.gaysorn.com | Skytrain: Chit Lom (direct access)*

INSIDER TIP MAH BOONKRONG (MBK)
(127 F1) (*m H4*)

Reasonable prices and flea market vibe every day. The Mah Boonkrong is one of the city's original shopping centres and is still a hit with the Thais. There are 1500 shops and stalls on seven floors. *Phaya Thai Rd | www.mbk-center.co.th | Skytrain: Siam Central (direct access)*

PLATINUM FASHION MALL
(123 D6) (*m J4*)

Their slogan is 'Thailand's largest Fashion Mall' and with about 1000 shops that sounds about right. However, it is a matter of quantity versus quality. You won't find valuable designer clothing here, but plenty clothes and accessories like shoes and toys – and everything for really low prices. This is also where you will find lots of wholesalers. Only a few steps further down the street is the *Grand Diamond Plaza (www.granddiamondplaza.com)* with similar bargains. *Pethburi Rd (shortly after the crossing with Ratchadamri Rd, on the way to Pantip Plaza) | www.platinumfashionmall.com | Saen Saep khlong boat: Pratunam | next Skytrain station: Chit Lom, 10 minutes on foot from there*

SIAM CENTER
(127 F1) (*ØØ H4*)

The centre, with its 120 shops, is very popular among the city's trendy youth. Right next door is the Siam Discovery Centre, which is even more popular. *Rama I Rd | www.siamcenter.co.th | Skytrain: Siam Central (direct access)*

SIAM PARAGON ★
(128 A1) (*ØØ H4*)

Exclusive and huge, it sells everything from Maseratis to Prada handbags. You will also find some popular Thai fashion labels like Flynow, Greyhound and Jaspal. A mega department store, a supermarket, 14 cinemas and South East Asia's largest aquarium also from part of this glamorous shopping world. You can eat at one of the 100 food stalls and restaurants, ranging from basic to super-elegant. *Rama I Rd | www.siamparagon.co.th | Skytrain: Siam Central (direct access)*

SILOM COMPLEX
(128 A4) (*ØØ H7*)

This is an all in one centre where you can buy everything from cameras to clothing, there are plenty of shops and a department store. *Silom Rd (near Patpong) | Skytrain: Sala Daeng | MRT: Silom*

GOLD & JEWELLERY

Thais invest their savings in 23 carat gold jewellery. The unit of weight is the baht (not to be confused with the national currency), which corresponds to 15.16 grams. The value of the article only increases by 10 per cent after processing. This pure gold (almost) is available only in special gold shops. The price varies according to the value of gold at the time. The centre for gold trading is located in Chinatown, especially in Yaowarat Road and in Charoen Krung Road.

Thailand is a centre for the production of gemstone jewellery but unfortunately there are many unscrupulous dealers in

A shopping world in itself: the luxurious Siam Paragon

the field who try to sell overpriced synthetic and worthless stones to tourists. An entire army of scam artists specialise in getting tourists into shops of this kind. If you are the victim of a scam, you can call the tourism police *(Hotline 1155)* but it is unlikely that you will get your money back. The jewellers in the shopping arcades of the expensive hotels are authentic businesses but of course the disadvantage is that you will pay much higher prices. You can have the gems valued at jewellery traders *(Thai Gem & Jewelry Traders Association | Jewelry Trade Center, 52th Floor | 919/616 Silom Rd | tel. 02 63 01 39 07 | www.thaigemjewelry.or.th | Skytrain: Sala Daeng | MRT: Silom).*

JOHNY'S GEMS
(120 C6) (*M C4*)

The exporter, wholesaler and retailer has been in business for over 50 years, stocks exquisitely designed jewellery and has a great reputation. *197–199 Fungnakorn Rd (side street of Charoen Krung Rd, near Wat Ratchabopit) | www.johnysgems.com | MRT: Hua Lampong, then 15 minutes by taxi*

INSIDER TIP ▸ **MATINA AMANITA**
(128 C1) (*M J4*)

The Thai designer Matina Sukhata creates the most fabulous jewellery, beautiful pieces that are all extremely feminine. Many of her creations are based on animal and flower motifs. *Gaysorn Plaza, Level B | Ploenchit Rd | www.matinaamanita.com | Skytrain: Station Chit Lom (direct access)*

UTHAI'S GEMS
(129 D2) (*M K5*)

A renowned jeweller that is noted for his creativity, even Nancy Reagan has bought gemstones here. *28/7 | Soi Ruam Ruedi (Seitenstraße der Ploenchit Rd) | Skytrain: Ploen Chit*

YVES JOAILLIER
(128 B4) (*M K7*)

This Frenchman has made a name for himself in Bangkok with his jewellery featuring modern designs. *Chan Issara Tower, 3rd Floor | 942/83 Rama IV Rd | Skytrain: Sala Daeng | MRT: Silom*

LOW BUDGET

▸ Street vendors do their shopping at the *Bo Beh Market* **(122 A5)** (*M F3*) where you can buy jeans or T-shirts for next to nothing. Items are usually sold in dozens, but if you ask for individual pieces, many of the dealers will oblige. *Krung Kasem Rd | Saen Saep khlong boat: Tha Charoenrat | Skytrain: National Stadium, then 5 minutes by taxi*

▸ Bangkok's shopping centres are constantly trying to attract custom by offering discounts, so check up on sale dates in the city newspapers, the 'Bangkok Post' and 'The Nation'.

▸ Thais change their mobile phones as quickly as their shirts. A large selection of used mobile phones are for sale on the 4th floor of the *Mah Boonkrong Centre (p. 72).*

DEPARTMENT STORES

CENTRAL CHITLOM ★
(128 C1) (*M K4*)

A store that is spread over six floors with an enormous selection of textiles, shoes, perfumes, household goods, toys, etc. On the seventh floor you can relax and enjoy a selection of international cuisine in the stylish *Foodloft. Ploenchit Rd | www.central. co.th | Skytrain: Chit Lom (direct access)*

ZEN (128 B1) (*M K4*)

This stylish department store, which was almost destroyed by fire during the politi-

The classic souvenir: decorative wood carvings at Narai Phand

cal unrest in 2010, was completely refurbished and reopened in 2011. A meeting point for trendsetters on the hunt for international and Thai designer fashions. *In Central World | Ratchadamri Rd | Skytrain: Chit Lom*

ARTS & CRAFTS

CABBAGES & CONDOMS HANDICRAFTS (129 F3) *(🛱 M5)*

Righ xext to the restaurant with the same name. When you shop here, you are doing good as the proceeds help to benefit, among other things, the fight against Aids. *Sukhumvit Rd, Soi 12 | Skytrain: Asok | MRT: Sukhumvit*

CHITRALADA SHOPS ⟳

These shops are a project under the auspices of Queen Sirkit. The Chitralada Foundation was created to help the poor rural population, specifically the housewives, to produce an extra income. Baskets, hand woven fabrics and textiles, handicrafts and souvenirs are distributed to the shops. *Branches: Oriental Place | Charoen Krung Rd, Soi 38 (near the Oriental Hotel) | express boat: Tha Oriental* (126 C5) *(🛱 E7) | Thaniya Plaza | Silom Rd | Skytrain: Sala Daeng* (128 A4) *(🛱 H7) | branches also at the Grand Palace, the Vimanmek Palace and at the airport*

INSIDER TIP METROPOLITAN MUSEUM OF ART STORE (128 A1) *(🛱 0)*

You can purchase miniature copies of antique artworks in the New York Metropolitan Museum's shop. The objects for sale range from Egyptian statues through to medieval jewellery to modern paintings. *Emporium Shopping Centre, 3rd floor | Sukhumvit Rd (at Soi 24) | Skytrain: Phrom Pong (direct access via Skywalk)*

MARKETS

NARAI PHAND ★
(128 C1) (🗺 J4)

The largest selection of arts and crafts in Thailand – ceramics, lacquer pieces, bronze and pewter ware, carvings – you can find everything and most items are even cheaper than you can buy from street vendors. The reason being that this is a collaboration between the government and the private sector to promote handicrafts. *Ratchadamri Rd (opposite Central World) | www.naraiphand.com | Skytrain: Chit Lom*

PRASSART COLLECTION
(128 B2) (🗺 J5)

This shop specialises in old and new Benjarong porcelain, distinctive for its flower decorations and five colours. *Peninsula Plaza | Ratchadamri Rd (at the Hotel Regent) | Skytrain: Chit Lom*

TAMNAN MINGMUANG

Whether terracotta statues, Benjarong porcelain or carvings – Tamnan Mingmuang's branches don't offer the usual tourist knick-knacks but rather carefully chosen arts and crafts. *Branches: Thaniya Plaza (Silom Rd)* (128 A4) *(🗺 H7) | Skytrain: Sala Daeng | MRT: Silom | Amarin Plaza (Ploenchit Rd)* (128 C1) *(🗺 J4) | Skytrain: Chit Lom*

INSIDER TIP THAI CRAFT FAIRS ☺
(0) (🗺 0)

The Thai Craft Association is particularly proud of their fair trade practices. They distribute handicrafts by artisans from all over the country which provide an extra income for wood carvers from the mountain villages in the north and silk weavers from the north-east. Regular trade fairs in the apartment and hotel complex at *Jasmine City Building* (programmes at *www.thaicraft.org*). *Sukhumvit Rd, Soi 23 | Skytrain: Asok | MRT: Sukhumvit*

MARKETS

CHATUCHAK WEEKEND MARKET ★
(0) (🗺 0)

Even if you do not want to buy anything, a visit to what purports to be the largest flea market in the world is a must. More than 15,000 stands and stalls guarantee a fascinating stroll. You will find simply everything here – cowboy hats and eccentric clothing, brass fans and bonsai trees, coffee pots, art and oddities, the useful and the curious. There are also

COUNTERFEIT CHAMPIONS

Rolex watches, Calvin Klein perfumes or 501 Levi jeans: every brand and status symbol can be bought cheaply in Bangkok. Of course they are not originals: the Thais are counterfeit champions and their knock-offs and copies can be found at every market and street vendor. Product piracy is also illegal in Thailand but while the vendors may not necessarily get into trouble with the local authorities, you may find yourself in hot water if you travel back home with pirated products. In the best case scenario you could have your items confiscated and in the worst case scenario you could face an extremely hefty fine from the authentic producers of the brand. You could be liable for fines of hundreds of pounds or dollars.

There is always space in your luggage for some bling from the night market in Patpong

many young Thai designers with their latest creations. This truly is a once in a lifetime experience! Tip: come as early as possible when it is not too hot and busy or come on a Friday night when there is a smaller market with about 500 stands between 6pm and midnight. *Sat/Sun 6am–6pm | Chatuchak Park | Phahonyothin Rd | www.chatuchak.org | Skytrain: Mo Chit | MRT: Chatuchak*

NAKHON KASEM
(126 A1) (*ⓜ D4*)
The 'thief's market' still lives off its old reputation but the times when you could buy back your stolen digital camera are long gone. Not a real market, but more of an amalgamation of shops and street vendors, who offer a collection of cheap electronic goods and other curiosities. *Chakrawat Rd (between Yaowarat and Chaoren Krung Rd in Chinatown) | MRT: Hua Lampong, then 10 minutes by taxi*

PAHURAT MARKET
(125 E1) (*ⓜ C5*)
Textile market in Little India. Whether you are looking for strong tweed from England, flowing silk from Japan or an Indian sari: you should be able to find them here. *Pahurat Rd | express boat: Tha Saphan Phut*

PAK KHLONG TALAD
(125 D2) (*ⓜ B5*)
Fruit, vegetables, flowers: the entire wealth of the tropics is delivered to this wholesale market by freight and it all begins a few hours before dawn. Have a morning coffee and freshly fried donut at one of the pavement stalls right on the river. *Maharat Rd (near Memorial Bridge) | express boat: Tha Rachini*

PATPONG NIGHT BAZAAR
(127 F4) (*H7*)

The popular night market in Patpong has all the souvenirs that you will find in any tourist district but everything here is a bit more expensive. But if you are looking for handbags, this is where you will find the city's widest selection of stands and shops. *Patpong 1 (side street of the Silom Rd) | Skytrain: Sala-Daeng | MRT: Silom*

PRATHUNAM MARKET (123 E5) (*J3*)

The textiles in this labyrinth of stalls are not quite as cheap as at the Bo Beh Market, but still a bargain. Wholesalers and retailers. *Ratchaphrarop Rd (at the Baiyoke Sky Hotel) | Saen Saep khlong boat: Tha Prathunam*

INSIDER TIP SIAM SQUARE
(128 A1) (*H4*)

Not an open air market but a warren of alleys opposite the Siam Centre with hundreds of shops that are as good as a fair. Many young designers sell their creations at reasonable prices to the hip young clientele. *Rama I Rd | Skytrain: Siam Central*

SIAM PARADISE NIGHT BAZAAR ★
(0) (*0*)

After years of debate, Bangkok's largest night market, the Suan Lum Night Bazaar at the Lumphini Park was torn down. Its successor is the Siam Paradise Night Bazaar, opened in 2011 – not quite as large as its predecessor, but it nevertheless has 1300 stalls and food stands. It is situated quite far from the centre, but is quick to get to by Skytrain from the On Nut station. *Daily 3pm–midnight | Sukhumvit Rd | Skytrain: Punnawithi*

TAILOR-MADE

A few guidelines: don't have your dress or suit tailored shortly before your trip

A tailor-made suit in Bangkok is a luxury you can afford

home. Agree on at least two fittings and so that you can change what you don't like. Don't pay upfront, but put down a deposit (about half) instead and be careful of tailors who have touts on the streets that promise a lot for very little money.

ART'S TAILOR
(127 F4) (*ℳ H7*)

An excellent men's tailor. Here you find that a custom-made suit can also cost a fortune, even in Bangkok. *62/15–6 Thaniya Rd (side street off Silom Rd) | Skytrain: Sala Daeng | MRT: Silom*

DINO (129 F2) (*ℳ M5*)

A reliable men and women's tailor. *Sukhumvit Rd (between Soi 10 and 12) | Skytrain: Nana | MRT: Sukhumvit*

NICKERMANN'S (129 E2) (*ℳ L5*)

The name sounds like a joke, but this tailor is highly reputable among foreigners living in Bangkok. *Landmark Hotel | 138 Sukhumvit Rd | www.nickermanns.net | Skytrain: Nana*

INSIDER TIP ▶ PINKY TAILOR ●
(129 D2) (*ℳ K5*)

Trading since 1980, with countless patrons and a great reputation. *884/40 Mahatun Plaza Arcade (behind the actual plaza) | Ploenchit Rd | www.pinkytailor.com | Skytrain: Ploen Chit*

FURNITURE

Many businesses will also organise the shipment of your purchases via sea freight. Hand-made furniture is cheaper here than back home – despite freight costs – and all are unique items.

GOLD BELL (0) (*ℳ 0*)

Furniture made out of teak and rosewood, also made to order. *720/15–17 Sukhumvit Rd (between Soi 28 and 30) | www.goldbell-furniture.com | Skytrain: Thong Lo*

PETER FURNITURE
(128 C2) (*ℳ J5*)

Has an excellent reputation with Bangkok's expats community and with the foreigners that work here. *Soi Mahadlek (side street off Ratchadamri Rd) | behind the Four Seasons Hotel | Skytrain: Chit Lom*

TIBET HOUSE
(126 C5) (*ℳ F7*)

Tibetan furniture and crafts from the Himalayas. *O. P. Place | Charoen Krung Rd, Soi 38 (near the Oriental Hotel) | express boat: Tha Oriental*

SILK

Original Thai silk is woven by hand and as such has many fine knots. '100% pure Thai silk' is offered at every corner, but for a few baht you will receive only synthetic or a blend of materials. If in doubt rather buy from the specialist shops which can be found along Silom, Surawong and Sukhumvit Roads.

SHINAWATRA
(0) (*ℳ 0*)

One of the largest silk producers in the country, with an excellent reputation. *Sukhumvit Rd, Soi 23 | www.tshinawatra.com | Skytrain: Asok | MRT: Sukhumvit*

JIM THOMPSON
(128 A4) (*ℳ H6*)

The most famous silk shop in Bangkok, a large selection of colours and some rather high prices. At the INSIDER TIP ▶ fabric sale up to 50 per cent cheaper. *9 Surawong Rd | www.jimthompson.com | MRT: Silom | Skytrain: Sala-Daeng | branches in the hotels Oriental and Westin and in Central World | factory outlet: 149/4–6 Surawong Rd*

ENTERTAINMENT

 **WHERE TO START?**

The hip and elegant clubs are spread across town while the red light district is concentrated around **Patpong**, **Nana Plaza** and **Soi Cowboy**. There are, however, streets with more stylish and classy bars and clubs. But if you don't want to travel far when bar-hopping, then stay around the tourist district of **Banglamphoo**: the party is always only a few steps away in the **Khao San Road** and its side alleys where even the Thais go to party.

Bangkok's nightlife is infamous. Dimly lit night clubs and massage parlours, go-go girls and Patpong's red light district have all given this city its dubious reputation. But aside from these shady establishments there are also the kinds of clubs, bars and trendy eateries that you would expect to find in major cities like London or New York.

In recent years the numbers of trendy bars, clubs and pubs have mushroomed and it is best to see what is what by looking at *www.bangkokgigguide.com* and *www.lastnightinbangkok.com*. A number of clubs have cover charges but the en-

Cocktail bars, clubs and cabaret: Bangkok's nightlife has more to offer than just go-go bars

trance fee usually includes one or two drinks. Night owls should beware: closing time for bars is 2am or 1am on the outskirts.

Every night Bangkok's largest bar district transforms itself into a night market, the *Patpong Night Bazaar*, which is so safe that you could happily stroll through with your mum. Bangkok at night is really not a dangerous city.

If, however, you are in the mood for the opera, a concert, the theatre or a ballet, then you have chosen the wrong city. While this sort of cultured entertainment is sometimes on offer, it is definitely not of the best. What would be considered highlights in Western culture are boring to most Thais. They prefer to have fun when going out at night which is why they would rather sing at a karaoke bar than listen to a symphony orchestra, and they would rather go to a boxing match than to a ballet.

ENTERTAINMENT DISTRICTS

KHAO SAN ROAD ●
(120 B–C4) (*ⓜ C2*)

The backpackers no longer have the Khao San Road to themselves as more and more clubbers venture there on their nights

Patpong. There have also been no reports of people being ripped-off here. *Sukhumvit Rd, Soi 4 (Soi Nana) | Skytrain: Nana*

PATPONG (128 A4) (*ⓜ H7*)

In Patpong, Bangkok's most famous bar mile, there are now more souvenir shops than go-go bars. The place swarms with tourists in flip-flops, but you really should to pay it a visit. But don't be taken in by the touts that will try to lure you into the

Bangkok club scene constantly reinvents itself and new bars open all the time

out. There are always new bars opening and each one is hipper and cooler than the last. It's party time every night on KSR.

NANA PLAZA (129 E2) (*ⓜ L5*)

One go-go bar after another on three floors around a courtyard. There are beer bars squashed next to each other in the open air and while the guests are mainly tourists, it is still not as touristy as in

shops on the top floor. Reputable establishments (like the bars from the King's Group) only have bouncers outside their doors. In the clubs on the street parallel to Patpong, *Soi 2 (Thaniya)*, is where you will find the Japanese, while the trendy bars in the narrow *Soi 4 (www.silomsoi4.net)* are full of stylish gays, but also women and heterosexuals are welcome here. *Silom Rd | Patpong | www.patpong*

nightlife.com | Skytrain: Sala Daeng | MRT: Silom

INSIDER TIP ► PHRA ATHIT ROAD
(120 B3) (*ﾑ B2*)

Pubs with live music, cafés and restaurants in buildings that are often more than a 100 years old. Khao San Road is not far, but it is mostly Thais and students from the nearby Thammasat University that come here. A very relaxed and pleasant atmosphere. *Chao Phraya express boat: Phra Athit*

ROYAL CITY AVENUE (0) (*ﾑ 0*)

The pubs, open air restaurants and cafés in this area are filled with young Thais. Live music and authentic Thai cuisine is available at Brown Sugar Café. As the RCA is a bit off the beaten track, not many tourists come here. *Royal City Avenue (parallel to New Petchburi Rd) | MRT: Phetburi, then 10 minutes by taxi*

INSIDER TIP ► SARASIN ROAD
(128 C3) (*ﾑ J–K6*)

The cafés, restaurants, bars and pubs that overlook Lumphini Park are not reliant on tourism and this is a popular place for Thais and expat locals. *Sarasin Rd | Skytrain: Ratchadamri*

SOI COWBOY (129 F2) (*ﾑ M5*)

Considerably quieter than Nana Plaza or Patpong, a side street with a few dozen beer and go-go bars. There are no touts or inflated bills, no scams. If you visit a few times in a row and sit on the same barstool, you will be considered a regular. *Sukhumvit Rd (between Soi 21 and Soi 23) | Skytrain: Asok | MRT: Sukhumvit*

INSIDER TIP ► SOI THONGLO (0) (*ﾑ 0*)

Many restaurants (some of which serve their guests Thai cuisine on the pavement after midnight) as well as pubs, clubs and karaoke bars. You will meet mostly Thais and expats, many of whom live in this area. The *Witch's Tavern*, an English pub with live music is popular with foreigners. *Sukhumvit Rd, Soi 55 (Thonglo) | Skytrain: Thong Lo*

BARS & CLUBS

BAMBOO BAR (126 C5) (*ﾑ E8*)

Opened in 1946, it is almost as much of an institution as the Hotel Oriental itself. With live jazz and a Thaijito cocktail (with local Mekong whiskey) in hand you will feel transported back to the time when writers like Somerset Maugham were here. Fans on the ceiling and couches with (fake) leopard skins give it an African

---

★ Bed Supperclub
The ultimate space shuttle to launch you into the nightlife
→ p. 84

★ Q Bar
The legend lives: exclusive bar with an endless cocktail menu
→ p. 85

★ Calypso Cabaret
A lavishly staged, fast-paced transvestite show → p. 86

★ 808 Bangkok
Mega club with elite international DJs → p. 86

★ Club Culture
Sound temple with room for 1000 revellers → p. 87

★ Siam Niramit
Old Siam in a fairy tale show
→ p. 87

MARCO POLO HIGHLIGHTS

feeling. *Sun–Thu 11pm–1am, Fri/Sat 11pm–2am | Oriental Hotel | 48 Oriental Avenue | tel. 0 26 59 90 00 | www.mandarinoriental.com | Skytrain: Saphan Taksin*

BAR SU (129 F2) *(ᗰ M5)*

This club, in the exclusive Sheraton Grande Sukhumvit, attracts the over 35 genera-tion who don't have to count every penny. Once you have filled up on wapas (rich tapas), it is time to hit the dance floor to some 70s and 80s rock. Gangsta rap and techno are taboo. *Daily 7pm –2am | 250 Sukhumvit Rd | www.barsubangkok.com | Skytrain: Asok*

INSIDER TIP BAY TA RA – BAR TA LE (120 B3) *(ᗰ C2)*

'Ta Le' means the ocean. You won't find that here in the tourist district of Banglamphoo, but there is a pool that you can dip into when the party gets too hot. Bands per-form every evening and delicious Thai food is served on the roof terrace. *Daily 6pm –1am | 149 Soi Ram Butri*

BED SUPPERCLUB ⭐ (129 E1) *(ᗰ M5)*

It looks like an all white spaceship. Stylish people lounge around on sofas and dine on the best Mediterranean-Asian fusion food. The calories can be danced off in the bar next door. Top international DJs with different sounds and events every day. No entry without a reservation and passport (or copy of passport)! *Daily 8pm –1am | 26 Sukhumvit Rd, Soi 11 | www.bedsupperclub | Skytrain: Nana*

INSIDER TIP BRICK BAR (120 B4) *(ᗰ C2)*

The best place for Bob Marley fans. Every evening there are live performances by three ska and reggae bands who take turns on stage. Even though the Brick Bar is situated in the middle of Banglamphoo, the backpacker district, and one of the most famous tourist hostels, it still at-tracts many Thais. *Daily 7pm –1.30am | Buddy Lodge | 265 Khao San Rd | www.brickbarkhaosan.com | Chao Phraya express boat: Phra Athit*

BROWN SUGAR (128 C3) *(ᗰ K6)*

An institution for jazz lovers with live ses-sions every evening from 9pm. Many locals and Westerners living in Bangkok come here, but few tourists. *Daily 7pm–1am | Soi Sarasin (at the Lumphini Park) | Skytrain: Ratchadamri*

DALLAS COWBOY PUB (128 A1) *(ᗰ H4)*

Wild West in Bangkok and naturally the live bands perform mainly country and western songs. The beer in the pub is cheap, the Thai cuisine is spicy and the clientele are usually students. *Daily 6pm–1am | 412 Siam Square, Soi 6 | tel. 0 22 55 32 76 | Skytrain: Siam Central*

LOW BUDGET

▶ *Happy Hour* in Bangkok's bars is usually from about 5pm to 8pm. Drinks cost 50 per cent less. Posters or bar bouncers will let you know which bars have a happy hour.

▶ *Cheap Charlie's* **(129 E2)** *(ᗰ M5)* the name says it all. The only place you will find cheaper beer is at the supermarket. The open air bar is an institution and a favourite among Western patrons. It is outside of the bar area but still in the middle of the tourist centre. *Daily 5pm–mid-night | Sukhumvit Rd, Soi 11 (across from the Ambassador Hotel) | Skytrain: Nana*

LONG TABLE ⚜
(129 F3) (𝄢 M6)

The long table with space for 70 people in this hip eatery is not the only attraction. The outdoor bar terrace with swimming pool on the 25th floor is perfect for sundowners or midnight Martini. The meet-

Lang Suan (near Sarasin Rd) | Skytrain: Ratchadamri

Q BAR ★ (129 E1) (𝄢 M4)

Infinite cocktail menu, international DJs and theme parties. Meeting place for stylish clubbers – slapdash outfits don't stand

Stylish guests: the Q Bar is a trendy hotspot for night owls

ing place for Bangkok's trendsetters. *Daily 5pm–2am | Column Building | Sukhumvit Rd, Soi 16 | www.longtablebangkok.com | Skytrain: Asok | MRT: Sukhumvit*

INSIDER TIP THE METAL ZONE
(128 C3) (𝄢 K6)

This is a rock music venue: heavy and trashy on the upper end of the decibel scale. If you have hair long and wear leather jackets (in the tropics) then this is the best place for you to test the quality of your earplugs. *Daily 8.30pm–1am | Soi*

a chance – with a chill out lounge and outside terrace. Entry only with passport (or a copy). *Daily 8pm–1am | Sukhumvit Rd, Soi 11 (at the lower end) | www.qbarbangkok.com | Skytrain: Nana*

RED SKY ⚜ (128 B1) (𝄢 J4)

A massive light blue rainbow shines over this rooftop bar and it sets the scene perfectly for a cocktail at dusk. Here the romantics are very close to heaven and all our earthly matters seem insignificant and trivial when looking down a distance of 200m/656ft. *Daily 5pm–1am | Centara Grand Hotel | Rama I Rd (at the shopping centre Central World) | www.centarahotels resorts.com | Skytrain: Chit Lom*

INSIDER TIP THE ROCK PUB
(122 C6) (*ω H3*)

The entrance looks like the gate to a robber baron's castle and inside it is all loud live rock. Top bands perform here as does Thailand's guitar legend, Lam Morrison, who regularly gigs here. *Daily 7pm–2am | Phaya Thai Rd (across from Asia Hotel) | www.therockpub-bangkok.com | Skytrain: Ratchathewi*

SAXOPHONE PUB & RESTAURANT
(123 D3) (*ω J1*)

Bangkok's very fickle night owls have remained loyal to this large complex for years (something not to be taken lightly). This is because both the Thai cuisine and the live music are excellent. Half a dozen bands perform every evening, playing everything from rock to salsa. *Daily 6pm–1am | 3/8 Phaya Thai Rd | Victory Monument | www.saxophonepub.com | Skytrain: Victory Monument*

INSIDER TIP TITANIUM CLUB & ICE BAR
(0) (*ω 0*)

This trendy nightspot is cool, hot and happening. Their resident band, *Unicorn*, is considered to be Thailand's hottest rock band. This may have something to do with them being an all girl band. To cool off there is the 'cool' Vodka bar where about 70 different kinds are served at minus 10 degrees. *Daily 6pm–1.30am | Sukhumvit Rd, Soi 22 | www.titanium bangkok.com | Skytrain: Asok, Phrom Pong*

V9 ☆ (127 E5) (*ω G7*)

A wine bar on the 37th floor of the Sofitel Silom Hotel that also features a first class restaurant. It has a spectacular panoramic view of the night city and the music is played at just the right volume making this the perfect venue for a romantic evening. *Daily 5pm–2am | 188 Silom Rd | www.sofitel.com | Skytrain: Chong Nonsi*

BEER GARDEN

SIAM PARADISE NIGHT BAZAAR
(0) (*ω 0*)

This night market is not only for shopping. Right in its midst is a beer garden with tables for 400 guests. There are enough live bands to keep you happy and they start playing in the late afternoon. *Daily 3pm–midnight | Sukhumvit Rd | Skytrain: Punnawithi*

CABARET

CALYPSO CABARET ★ ●
(122 C5) (*ω H3*)

The ladyboys put on a fast-paced drag show. Every night professional and talented artists present a very entertaining revue. The show has an international director and features opulent costumes and sophisticated staging and choreography. *Daily 8.15pm and 9.45pm | admission fee 1200 baht (online registration only 900 baht) | Asia Hotel | Phya Thai Rd | tel. 0 26 53 39 60 | www.calypsocabaret.com | Skytrain: Ratchathewi*

DISCO & DANCING

808 BANGKOK ★ (0) (*ω 0*)

DJs from all over the world fly in to mix their beats in this cool, stylish mega club which plays a variety of styles from reggae to underground hip hop. The light and sound system is pretty much the best that Bangkok's nightlife has to offer. *Daily 9pm–2am | Royal City Avenue, Block C | tel. 0 26 22 25 72 | www.808bangkok.com | arrival by taxi*

THE CLUB (120 C4) (*C2*)

The old Khao San haunt has been completely refurbished and is once again the most popular party destination on the backpacker mile. The masters at the turntables play techno, house, breakbeats and drum 'n' bass while the laser sends a lightning show through crowds of dancers. *Sun–Tue 10pm–2am, Fri/Sat 8pm–2am | 123 Khao San Rd | tel. 0 26 29 22 55 | www.theclubkhaosan.com | Saen Saep khlong boat: Tha Phanfa*

CLUB CULTURE ★ (123 D4) (*J2*)

This place has been a late night bar, restaurant and a theatre. It is now a sound temple with enough room for 1000 party animals. Whether it is house, techno or hip hop – everyone is catered for here. *Tue–Sun 9pm–2am | Sri Ayutthaya Rd (across Siam City Hotel) | tel. 0 26 53 72 16 | www.club-culture-bkk.com | Skytrain: Phaya Thai*

CONCEPT CM² (128 A1) (*H4*)

Five discos and bars (*La Femme* is ladies only) at the Novotel Hotel and live music every evening. *Daily 7pm–2am | Siam Square, Soi 6 | tel. 0 22 55 68 88 | www.cm2bkk.com | Skytrain: Siam Central*

LUCIFER (128 A4) (*H7*)

The devil watches from a glowing red mask as the ravers dance to 'infernally' loud music. Even though it is in the middle of Patpong, you will also see lots of pierced young Thais with an affinity for trendy Western techno music. *Daily 8pm–2am | Patpong 1 | tel. 0 22 34 69 02 | Skytrain: Sala Daeng | MRT: Silom*

THEATRE

SIAM NIRAMIT ★ (0) (*0*)

Bangkok's largest show spectacular: 150 actors in a 40 million dollar theatre take

Drag show at the Calypso

2000 visitors on a fairy tale trip through the kingdom of Siam and its history. The show's complex includes four traditional Thai villages and a 700-seater restaurant. *Daily 6–10pm, show 8pm | admission fee from 1500 baht | 19 Tiam Ruammit Rd | tel. 0 26 49 92 22 | www.siamniramit.com | MRT: Thailand Cultural Centre (shuttle bus from there)*

THAILAND CULTURAL CENTRE (0) (*0*)

The Bangkok Symphony Orchestra plays here and it is also the stage for traditional Thai performances. Occasionally you can see performances of operas, ballets and concerts by foreign ensembles. Information can be found in the newspapers or by enquiring. *Ratchadaphisek Rd | tel. 0 22 47 00 28 | www.culture.go.th | MRT: Thailand Cultural Centre*

WHERE TO STAY

Finding a bed in Bangkok is not a problem and even if you want to stay in five star luxury accommodation and you can easily do so without spending a small fortune. Compared other top international destinations, you will definitely get your money's worth in Bangkok.

Some of the world's best luxury hotels are here in Thailand's capital city. And even in these temples of hospitality you can get a room key – these days they are often chip cards – from about 6800 baht upwards.

There is very little price difference between a single and a double room and for as little as 4000 baht you can expect quite a few luxuries and the same goes for hotels that charge between 2000 and 40,000 baht per night.

A swimming pool, a fridge, TV, telephone and of course air-conditioner are all standard in hotels that charge between 1000 and 2000 baht per room and even if you pay less than 1000 baht per night, you can expect a decent room that is equipped with TV, fridge, telephone and air-conditioner. In basic guest houses you can have a good night's rest for as little as 40 baht.

The better hotels add a 10 per cent service charge and 7 per cent VAT on to the room rate and the rate at the top hotels can

Photo: The Oriental

In Bangkok you can stay in luxury at a top hotel or choose a comfortable guest house, either way you will get excellent value for your money

differ greatly according to season, with the highest prices being charged in high season between November and February. You should certainly pre-book if travelling in mid-December through to mid-January. There is a counter for the Thai hotel consortium *(www.thaihotels.org)* at the arrival hall at the airport in Bangkok.
You will find hotel reviews online at *www.travelfish.org*.

HOTELS: EXPENSIVE

BAIYOKE SKY HOTEL
(123 E5) *(J3)*
Thailand's tallest hotel (309m/1013ft), at the Prathunam Market is ideally located for shopping. It is not to be mistaken with the Baiyoke Suite Hotel, right next door, that is half its size. Spacious, very comfortably furnished rooms with great views.

The Shangri-La Hotel complex: a luxurious oasis

660 rooms | 222 Ratchaphrarop Rd | tel. 0 26 56 30 00 | www.baiyokehotel.com | Saen Saep khlong boat: Tha Prathunam

DREAM HOTEL ★
(129 F2) (*M5*)

A very hip hotel that is a five minute walk from Sukhumvit Road. By creating sophisticated lighting effects, it captivates cool elegance and is a perfect example of modern hotel architecture with an artistic touch. The hotel has a twin, there is one on each side of the street. Both hotels present a futuristic dream world with Asian flair. Fashion photographers like to use the foyer as a set for their fashion shoots. Swimming pool, gym and spa. 195 rooms | Sukhumvit Rd, Soi 15 | tel. 0 22 54 85 00 | www.dreambkk.com | Skytrain: Asok | MRT: Sukhumvit

DUSIT THANI (128 B4) (*J7*)

The luxurious flagship of the Thai Dusit chain remains consistent as one of Bangkok's top hotels. The hotel offers several first class restaurants (e.g. Thai, Vietnamese or Western) and both Lum-phini Park – superb for joggers – and the entertainment hub of Patpong, are at your doorstep. The hotel also offers the convenience of a spa, gym and driving range with its own golf professionals. 530 rooms | 946 Rama IV Rd | tel. 0 22 36 99 99 | www.dusit.com/dusit-thani | Skytrain: Sala Daeng | MRT: Lumphini

THE EUGENIA ★ (0) (*0*)

The nostalgic among you will be transported back in time as soon as you arrive in Thailand: guests are collected from the airport in a vintage Mercedes. The colonial mansion has massive wooden floors and the rooms feature antique furnishings and copper baths. The swimming pool in the courtyard is surrounded by palms and is a relaxation oasis. 12 rooms | Sukhumvit Rd, Soi 31 | tel. 0 22 59 90 11 | www.theeugenia.com | Skytrain: Phrom Phong (free shuttle service)

INSIDER TIP ▶ GRAND PRESIDENT
(129 E1) (*M5*)

The spacious apartments offer every comfort and even include kitchenettes. Three swimming pools, a gym, spa and sauna are also available. The overall quality and standard of service make this an excellent value for money option. *437 rooms | Sukhumvit Rd, Soi 11 | tel. 0 26 51 12 00 | www.grandpresident.com | Skytrain: Nana*

REMBRANDT HOTEL
(129 F3) (*M6*)

It need not be the impressive (2750ft²) presidental suite because even the smaller rooms have the same standards of luxury and comfort. Large swimming pool, spa, fitness centre and restaurants (Thai, Indian, Italian, Mexican), which are among the best in Bangkok. On a quiet side street near the Emporium shopping centre and nightlife (Soi Cowboy). *407 rooms | 19 Sukhumvit Rd, Soi 18 | tel. 0 22 61 71 00 | www.rembrandtbkk.com | Skytrain: Asok | MRT: Sukhumvit*

SEVEN ⭐ (0) (*0*)

Quite a few of the smaller establishments in Bangkok are called 'boutique' hotels but Seven does actually deserve the boutique label. It only has six rooms but each one is uniquely designed and combines modern design with traditional Thai themes. The 'seventh heaven' is the foyer with its all in red bar where young artists regularly exhibit their work. No restaurant, but there are many restaurants in the area. *6 rooms | Sukhumvit Rd, Soi 31, side alley 3/15 Sawasdee 1 | tel. 0 22 62 09 51 | www.sleepatseven.com | Skytrain: Phrom Phong*

SHANGRI-LA ⭐
(126 C6) (*E8*)

At first glance the name seems inappropriate: what does a massive hotel complex have to do with paradise? But its ambience and service means that it truly deserves the comparison. The same applies to the rooms, the restaurants as well as the exclusive spa, where you can relax with yoga exercises. *747 rooms, 52 suites | 89 Soi Charoen Krung 42/1 (Soi Wat Suan Plu) | tel. 0 22 36 77 77 | www.shangri-la.com/bangkok | Skytrain: Saphan Taksin*

SIAM@SIAM ⭐ ☼
(122 B6) (*G4*)

Carpets and raw concrete, weathered wood and bright colours – this unique hotel is the manifestation of avant-garde Thai design. It is an original and you will either love it or hate it. Whilst having a massage in the spa you can watch footballers in the national stadium opposite you. An absolute must is a visit to the *Skydine Restaurant* on the 25th floor with its panoramic view. And right on the top of the roof there is a full moon party every month. *203 rooms | 865 Rama I Rd | tel. 0 22 17 30 00 | www.siamatsiam.com | Skytrain: National Stadium*

⭐ **Dream Hotel**
East meets West: brave, futuristic design with an Asian atmosphere and lots of high tech → p. 90

⭐ **The Eugenia**
Travel in a vintage Mercedes to a boutique hotel with colonial flair → p. 90

⭐ **Seven**
You will be in seventh heaven in this colourful six-roomed boutique hotel → p. 91

⭐ **Siam@Siam**
A designer hotel that combines all the arts, the perfect place for a full moon party → p. 91

MARCO POLO HIGHLIGHTS

TRIPLE TWO SILOM
(127 E5) (𝄞 G7)

This establishment is a small exclusive sister hotel to the Narai Hotel next door (guests can use the pool). It is a stylish and modern boutique hotel with that is elegant, simple and very trendy. A culinary highlight is the buffet with the Vietnamese tapas at the *Triple Two Restaurant*. *75 rooms | 222 Silom Rd | tel. 0 26 27 22 22 | www.tripletwosilom.com | Skytrain: Chong Nonsi*

ZENITH SUKHUMVIT ☘
(129 E1) (𝄞 L4)

Comfortable rooms that are value for money, with mini bar, safe and TV, and you can even make your own coffee. Gym and spa and from the swimming pool on the 19th floor, you have a wonderful view over the city. At the hotel foyer's café, the INSIDER TIP ▶ *Baker's Dozen* there is a large selection of pastries and tarts from their own bakery. It's only a few steps to the Sukhumvit tourist mile. *160 rooms |*

LUXURY HOTELS

Metropolitan (128 C5) (𝄞 J7)

Like its sister hotel in London, this elegant establishment is also a perfect example of modern architecture. Dark wooden floors, white walls, clear lines and interesting lighting make it a real star. The two restaurants are top class, in ☺ *Glow* wellness is a top priority in the kitchen. A yoga studio, a spa with steam room and a swimming pool. Double rooms from 8600 baht, specials are considerably cheaper. *171 rooms, 5 suites with butler service | 27 South Satorn (Tai) Rd | tel. 0 26 25 33 33 | www.metropolitan.bangkok.como.bz | MRT: Lumphini*

The Oriental ☘ (126 C5) (𝄞 E8)

This is one of Bangkok's most famous hotels and it is regularly voted as one of the best hotels in the world. This luxury establishment has seen many famous guests, from pop stars to heads of state, and you can expect every imaginable luxury. And it overlooks the river of kings, the Chao Phraya. If you want just a little taste of the atmosphere then the best time for a visit is for afternoon tea in the *Author's Lounge* – but you should dress elegantly. Double rooms from 10,800 baht. *361 rooms, 35 suites | 48 Oriental Avenue | tel. 0 26 59 90 00 | www.mandarinoriental.com/bangkok | Skytrain: Saphan Taksin*

The Sukhothai (128 C5) (𝄞 J7)

A top class hotel, impressively elegant in simple Thai style. If you only want to have a look then go for their *Sunday Brunch (Sun midday–3pm)*. The gigantic buffet (2200 baht) offers the best Thai, Western and Japanese cuisine. Exclusive restaurants, large pool, Jacuzzi, sauna, aerobics, squash, tennis. The only (small) disadvantage is its location in the embassy district. You have to walk about 30 minutes to shop in Silom Road. But then again those who stay here do not need to ask about the cost of the hotel limousine. Double rooms from 7400 baht, specials from 7800 baht. *113 rooms, 44 suites | 13/3 South Satorn (Tai) Rd | tel. 0 23 44 88 88 | www.sukhothai. com | MRT: Lumphini*

29/117 Sukhumvit Rd, Soi 3 | tel. 0 26 55 49 99 | www.zenith-hotel.com | Skytrain: Nana | MRT: Sukhumvit

HOTELS: MODERATE

CITADINES SUKHUMVIT 11
(129 E1) (*M5*)

This is the fourth and youngest establishment in the Citadines Group, it is situated in a Sukhumvit side street (the others you will find in Soi 8, 16 and 23). It has large, modern apartments with kitchenettes and is another excellent value for money option. With swimming pool and gym. *127 rooms | Sukhumvit Rd, Soi 11 | tel. 0 22 64 67 77 | www.citadines.com | Skytrain: Nana*

CITICHIC
(129 F1) (*M5*)

Comfortable hotel on a quiet side street in the bustling tourist district. A lot of light and colours in the foyer, pastel tones and understated elegance in the rooms. Rooftop swimming pool and gym. *37 rooms | Sukhumvit Rd, Soi 13 | tel. 0 23 42 38 88 | www.citichichotel.com | Skytrain: Asok, Nana*

DAVINCI (0) (*0*)

Spacious, comfortable rooms, each individually decorated in an understated style. When you stay here you feel as though you are in a private home. Very good value for money. Restaurant with Thai and Italian cuisine. In the spa you can enjoy a massage or try an indulgent milk bath. *15 rooms | Sukhumvit Rd, Soi 31, side alley 3/8 Sawasdee | tel. 0 22 60 39 39 | www.davincilespa.com | Skytrain: Phrom Phong*

GRAND CHINA PRINCESS ✵
(125 F1) (*D5*)

The best establishment in Chinatown, about halfway between the Grand Palace and the shopping area in Silom Road. With a swimming pool and restaurants serving Western, Chinese and Japanese cuisine. Only a few Western tourists stay here, but this is a comfortable place for everyone who would like to stay in a hotel that is very Asian. *155 rooms | 215 Yaowarat Rd | tel. 0 22 24 99 77 | www.grandchina.com | MRT: Hua Lampong, then 10 minutes by taxi*

Sleek and stylish: the Metropolitan

INDRA REGENT
(123 E5) (*J3*)

Time has taken its toll on this once reputable hotel in the middle of the vibrant clothing markets of Prathunam. However, its price and performance are right. With swimming pool, gym and tennis court and it is only a 10-minute walk to the shopping district around Central World. *439 rooms | 120/126 Ratchaphrarop Rd |*

tel. 0 22 08 00 22 | www.indrahotel.com | Skytrain: Chit Lom, then 15 minutes by foot

INSIDER TIP ► **NAVALAI RIVER RESORT** ☀️ **(120 B3)** *(🌐 B2)*

The rooms are all decorated in warm colours and come with a TV, DVD, a safe and fridge. Tip: treat yourself to a room on the river side of the hotel and you will have the Chao Phraya at your feet when you are on your balcony. You also have a stunning view from the rooftop swimming pool and from the *Aquatini Restaurant* on the riverbank. *74 rooms | 45/1–2 Phra Athit Rd | tel. 0 22 80 99 55 | www.navalai.com | Chao-Phraya express boat: Tha Phra Athit*

SILOM CITY HOTEL (127 D5) *(🌐 G7)*

Here the standard is higher than the price. Very comfortable and spacious rooms with TV, safe, mini bar. No swimming pool, but a gym. About halfway between Chao Phraya and Patpong bar area in the Silom tourist district with many shopping opportunities. *70 rooms | Soi 72 Prachum (Silom, Soi 22) | between Silom and Surawong Rd | tel. 0 26 35 62 11 | www.silom cityhotel.com | Skytrain: Chong Nonsi*

INSIDER TIP ► **SOLO (129 E2)** *(🌐 L5)*

Simple elegance and all the comforts, on a quiet side street of the tourist centre on Sukhumvit Road. Opened in 2010, the

BOOKS & FILMS

► **Bangkok Then and Now** – this coffee-table book by Steve Van Beek (2001) shows the dramatic changes in the city over the past century with the use of comparative photographs.

► **Nana Plaza** – the bar district forms the backdrop of Christopher Moore's thriller (1999). The private detective Vincent Calvino, not averse to the odd drink, delves into its underworld.

► **Private Dancer** – nightmare in Bangkok, Stephen Leather describes how the relationship between a travel writer and a barmaid turns into a catastrophe (2005).

► **The King and I** – filmed four times, but the version with Yul Brynner as the King of Siam is still the best. Shot in 1956 by director Walter Lang it was set in the 19th century and concerned the adventures of the English govern-ess Anna (Deborah Kerr), who was responsible for the king's 58 children. In Thailand this film is banned (as is the 1999 version with Jodie Foster) as royalty have to be presented with the utmost respect.

► **Ong Bak** – Tony Jaa is an actor, kick boxer and superstar in Thailand. Director Prachya Pinkaew filmed this cult movie (2003). After chasing after a stolen Buddha head, Tony anni-hilates all his enemies. With English subtitles.

► **The Man with the Golden Colt** – James Bond (Roger Moore) has also been to Bangkok and he did it like the Thais do: he ignored the traffic rules. After a wild car chase through the city, the action moves to southern Thailand where he guns down Scaramanga, the bad guy played by Christopher Lee (1974, director: Guy Hamilton).

On a quiet side alley off Sukumvit Road: the Atlanta Hotel's foyer

hotel offers excellent value for money. On the rooftop there is *Bar Cloud 9* and a pool with a view over Bangkok's cityscape of high-rise buildings. *42 rooms | Sukhumvit Rd, Soi 2 | tel. 0 26 56 78 50 | www.solo hotelsresorts.com | Skytrain: Nana, Ploen Chit*

SWISS PARK HOTEL ☼
(129 E2) *(ω M5)*

The foyer of the hotel is not much to write home about, but you will be very comfortable in the rooms which are all equipped with TV, fridge and telephone. The hotel also has a small swimming pool and makes an impression with its prime location in the middle of the tourist district. Shopping and nightlife (Nana Plaza) are on your doorstep, and the motorway to the airport is just around the corner. *108 rooms | Sukhumvit Rd, Soi 11 | tel. 0 22 54 02 28 | www.swissparkhotelbangkok.com | Skytrain: Nana | MRT: Sukhumvit*

VIENGTAI HOTEL ☼
(120 C4) *(ω C2)*

The best hotel in the Banglamphoo backpacker area, with comfortable rooms with TV, telephone and even a swimming pool. The Khao San Road is only a few minutes on foot. *200 rooms | 42 Tani Rd | tel. 0 22 80 54 34 | www.viengtai.co.th | Saen Saep khlong boat: Tha Phanfa*

HOTELS: BUDGET

ATLANTA HOTEL (129 E2) *(ω L5)*

This traditional hostel is situated in a quiet side alley. Management makes every effort to make sure that the clientele are respectable and that nothing immoral or illegal takes place here. The simple rooms are spacious and clean, and there is a small tropical garden with a swimming pool. *49 rooms | 78 Sukhumvit Rd, Soi 2 | tel. 0 22 52 60 69 | www.theatlantahotel bangkok.com | Skytrain: Nana, Ploen Chit*

BANGKOK CHRISTIAN GUEST HOUSE
(128 B5) (*ɰ J7*)

No one asks you about your religious persuasion here. This well maintained and quiet guest house (no smoking) has simple rooms with air-conditioning and TV. Despite this, it may not be suitable for everyone. If you chose this place for the bars – Patpong is only a few minutes away – you might want to think again. There is a children's playground, a library and a chapel. The most reasonably priced accommodation in the area. *57 rooms | 123 Saladaeng Rd, Soi 2 | tel. 0 22 33 63 03 | www.bcgh.org | Skytrain: Sala Daeng | MRT: Silom*

D & D INN (120 C4) (*ɰ C2*)

One of the better bed and breakfast addresses in the area. Rooms with air-conditioner and TV, some also with a fridge. There is also a swimming pool. *65 rooms | 68–70 Khao San Rd | tel. 0 26 29 05 26 | www.khaosanby.com | Saen Saep khlong boat: Tha Phanfa*

KHAO SAN PALACE HOTEL
(124 C4) (*ɰ C2*)

After renovations this Khao San original changed its name from an 'inn' to a 'hotel'. All rooms are equipped with air-conditioning, TV/DVD and safe. The hotel is a reasonable distance from the famous street. From the small ⚲ swimming pool on the roof (7th floor) there is a beautiful view of the of the city's high-rise buildings. *100 rooms | 139 Khao San Rd | tel. 0 22 82 05 78 | www.khaosanpalace.com | Saen Saep khlong boat: Tha Phanfa*

MALAYSIA HOTEL
(129 D5) (*ɰ K8*)

Aside from the Atlanta, this is one of the oldest budget hotels in Bangkok. It is also popular with the older, more conventional crowd i.e. those with suitcases. The spacious, air-conditioned rooms are equipped with TV and fridge. With swimming pool and near the shopping area (Silom Road), the nightlife and Lumphini Park. *120 rooms | 54 Ngam Duphli Rd | Rama IV Rd | tel. 0 26 79 71 28 | www.malaysiahotelbkk.com | MRT: Lumphini*

NEW WORLD CITY HOTEL
(120 C3) (*ɰ C2*)

This hotel is one of the better ones in Banglamphoo. The air-conditioned rooms are furnished simply, but are spacious and come with a TV and fridge. Very conveniently located, it is a mere five minutes to the Khao San Road, another ten to the Grand Palace. *171 rooms | 2 Samsen Rd | tel. 0 22 81 55 96 | www.newworldcityhotel.com | Saen Saep khlong boat: Tha Phanfa (then 20 minutes on foot)*

LOW BUDGET

▶ Even on the supposedly expensive Sukhumvit Road, you can find very reasonably priced accommodation: in the relaxed *Suk 11 Hostel* **(129 E2)** *(ɰ M5)* there are basic rooms (with air-conditioning) from 500 baht. *80 rooms | 1/33 Sukhumvit Rd, Soi 11 (across from the Ambassador Hotel) | tel. 0 22 53 59 27 | www.suk11. com | Skytrain: Nana*

▶ Hotel per mouse click: many hotels offer discounts if you book via their website. But hotel and travel representatives also offer prices lower than the official rate so it is worth making comparisons, for example at *www.asiarooms.com*, *www.bangkok-hotel.ws* (with reviews) and *www.latestays.com*

INSIDER TIP ▶ RIVER VIEW GUEST HOUSE
(126 B3) (*m E6*)

Lodgings on the Chao Phraya in Chinatown that has clean rooms with fans or air-conditioners, some with fridge and TV, all individually decorated. Especially recommended are the balcony rooms on the riverbank. On the roof terrace: ✳️ restaurant and bar with great view. In the evenings you can even practise t'ai chi

retain its personal touch and it is in a great location near to the Grand Palace and National Museum. With swimming pool and a restaurant that is popular with both Thais and tourists *(Budget)*. *The Royal Hotel is the largest hotel near these historical sites. 297 rooms | 2 Ratchadamnoen Klang | tel. 0 22 22 91 11 | www.visit-mekong.com/royal-hotel | MRT: Hua Lampong, then 15 minutes by taxi*

For Asian flair at reasonable rates: the D & D Inn is the right choice

and qigong (also for non-guests). 34 rooms | 768 Soi Panu Rangsee, Song Wat Rd | tel. 0 22 34 54 29 | www.riverviewbkk. com | MRT: Hua Lamphong, 5 minutes from there by taxi | Chao Phraya express boat: Harbour Department, 15 minutes from there on foot

ROYAL HOTEL
(120 B4) (*m B3*)

Once a first class hotel, it has now seen better days but it has still managed to

INSIDER TIP ▶ SLEEP WITHINN
(120 C4) (*m C2*)

For tourists who like their comforts this is an excellent destination in Banglamphoo, the backpacker district. The six floor establishment offers tastefully decorated rooms equipped with air-conditioner, TV, safe and fridge. There is also a small swimming pool on the roof. *60 rooms | 76 Rambuttri Rd | tel. 0 22 80 30 70 | www.sleepwithinn.com | Saen Saep khlong boat: Tha Phanfa*

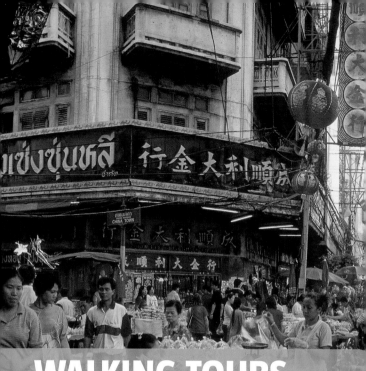

WALKING TOURS

The tours are marked in green in the street atlas, the pull-out map and on the back cover

1 WHERE THE FIRST EUROPEANS LIVED

The area around the Oriental Hotel at the Chao Phraya is called the 'old falang quarter' by city historians, a district of Western foreigners. Europeans built embassies and trading houses here in the 19th century. What they left behind and what has changed there is what you will discover on this hour-long walk.

Start at the colonial style Oriental Hotel → p. 92, this old building is in itself an example of the Bangkok's European past. Turn away from the river and stroll through Oriental Lane, a side street (Soi 40) of Charoen Krung Road. After a few steps you will see the Assumption Cathedral. The church was built in 1910 in a neo-Romanesque style and the marble altar was imported from France. They have an English sermon every Sunday at 10am. The Assumption College next to the church is considered to be the most prestigious Catholic university in the country.

Back on Soi 40, turn into the first alley to the left and you will come to Soi 38. You can't miss the O. P. Place. This shopping centre, in colonial style, is in itself quite eye-catching. On sale here are some rather pricy artworks and antiques. Right across

Photo: Chinatown

A maze of narrow alleyways and a peaceful oasis of calm: explore old Bangkok off the beaten track

from it is a 100-year old shop that is now an excellent Thai restaurant INSIDER TIP ▶ *Tongue Thai (daily 11am–2pm, 5pm–10.30pm | Soi 38, Charoen Krung Rd | tel. 0 26 30 99 18 | Moderate)*. The paintings on the walls of the wonderfully restored building are for sale as are the ceramics in the shelves. Even if you are not very hungry: the banana flower salad is a light and delicious snack.

From Soi 38 you turn left to the next parallel alley, Soi 36. Take another left towards the river where you pass two colonial style buildings, which are hidden behind a wall for security reasons: the **French Embassy** and the **Ambassador's Residence**, both dating from the middle of the 19th century. In front of you on the river you will see another weathered colonial building: the **Customs House**. This was the old toll building where trading ships used to declare their goods. Today the site is a station for fire engines and is also sometimes used as a set for movies. Scenes from the movie The Killing Fields about the Cambodian civil war were shot here in 1984.

Now it is back up Soi 36 where you will see a signpost on the left over an alley, which directs you to the Haroon Mosque and a cemetery. A network of tiny alleys spreads through the small Muslim district, where people still live today in their traditional wooden houses. The alleys are not on any maps, but you cannot get lost. Just look up every now and then: the turquoise-gray high-rise building, the CAT tower (Communications Authority of Thailand), points the way to the north and to Soi 34. If you walk back towards the river again, you will get to Wat Muang Kae. This monastery is not a tourist attraction, but with its old wooden buildings and the small temple it is worth having a look.

From the monastery pier (Tha Wat Muang Kae) a canal boat will take you back to the Oriental Hotel in a few minutes. If you have enough energy left, you can drive two piers further upstream, to Tha River City, and take the MARCO POLO city walk No. 2 from here.

2 FROM THE HOLY ROSARY CHURCH TO CHINA AND INDIA

Bangkok was founded at the banks of Chao Phraya and was very soon became a cosmopolitan capital city. The Portuguese, Chinese and Indians were early settlers. This walk takes a good two hours during which you will discover the city's interesting multi-ethnic past and present.

The action begins at the River City Shopping Complex → p. 71, Bangkok's largest shopping centre for antiques and handicrafts. A short distance north of it you will see a signpost, 'Walking Street to Chinatown' and the spire of the Holy Rosary Church, which is called Wat Kalawa in Thai. The original church on this site was built by the Portuguese in 1767, the present church was built in the Gothic style towards the end of the 19th century. There are no English sermons, but Mass is read in Thai *(Mon–Sat 6am and 7.30pm, Sun 8am and 7.30pm)* and in Chinese *(Sun 10am).*

A few steps further north, on the narrow Phanit Charoen Road is the Marine Department. The harbour master's office in itself is of little interest, but all around you the old China is still alive. Here you will see the typical 'shop-houses' where extended families live upstairs whilst the business takes up the downstairs area. There are quite a lot of dealers in spare vehicle parts around here and the area is not very appealing at first glance but do not fear, is it quite safe. Nothing will happen to you here, and even if there are only a few strangers walking along this route, no one will make you feel uncomfortable. If you see a lot of locals gathered around a wonky table, take a seat as it is quite likely that you will be served some very tasty duck with rice which will only cost you few baht.

Continue upstream and keep on the road, until you reach Soi Phanu Rangsee. Take this alley until you get to the River View Guest House → p. 97. As the name implies, you will have a lovely view over the river here. Enjoy a drink on the comfortable roof terrace and relax and watch all the activity on the Chao Phraya.

Now you can return via Soi Phanu Rangsee to Song Wat Road. You will be in the middle of Chinatown → p. 38. Along the Song Wat there may not be any tourist sites, but there is a piece of Bangkok –

No matter how crowded and narrow Chinatown's streets are, scooters will find a way through

away from the traffic jams – where time seems to stand still. Here you will see rice and spice traders waiting for their customers in their shops and warehouses that face the street – just as they have done for centuries. Glance upwards now and then and you will see the detail with which these houses were built. Even if the plaster on the walls is crumbling, the house fronts with their ornamental decorations, are still a marvellous example of the Sino-Portuguese building style, which shaped the architectural style of old Bangkok.

After about 800m you will come to an intersection with Ratchawong Road, take a right turn. After a few minutes you will reach the Sampeng Lane → p. 39. This whole area is a hive of activity and it has been this way since the Chinese began their shopping and bargaining here in the time of King Rama I. You will get an impressive view of the colourful hustle and bustle when you walk up the left section to Chakrawat Road. It is a little quieter here and after two minutes turn left towards the river and here, in Buddha's shadow at the Wat Chakrawat → p. 40, you will be able to breathe properly once again.

From the monastery go back onto the Chakrawat Road, cross over on the footbridge on your left to the other side street into Soi Bhopit Phimuk. In this alley it smells like cinnamon, pepper and all kinds of different spices. When you go over the bridge and the Ong An canal, you will come to a block of flats. Go to your left to Chakpetch Road.

The scent of patchouli, women in saris and turbaned Sikhs will make you think that you are in Bombay and not in Bangkok. This is Pahurat → p. 38, the Little India of the capital, which is famous for its textile shops. In Pahurat there are no amazing tourist attractions but as is the case with Chinatown, just about everything here is worth seeing. Just stroll around and do not worry about getting lost because despite the maze of alleys, it is really easy find your way around. One landmark, however, is the Sikh temple Sri Guru Singh Sabha → p. 40 with its golden dome on Chakpetch Road. Unfortunately it is encircled by so many buildings that you cannot see the façade at all. Right next door is the food paradise of the India Emporium where you can taste authentic Indian cuisine. In Pahurat Road plenty of shops sell splendid classical Thai dance costumes and matching masks.

About 15 minutes on foot south of Pahurat is the Chao Phraya where you can step onto a canal boat (e.g. at the pier Tha Saphan Phut) and travel further upstream to the Grand Palace → p. 29 (Tha Chang jetty).

3 TEMPLES OF TRANQUILLITY IN THE HEART OF THE OLD CITY

Temples are oases of calm amid the chaos of Bangkok. Go for a walk through the heart of the old city and discover some temples that you will not have to share with busloads of other tourists. Allow yourself about three hours and start your tour at Wat Pho.

The temple monastery Wat Pho → p. 33 with its reclining Buddha is one of the city's main sightseeing attractions and is always busy. But only a few minutes away you have a temple all for yourself: if you take Taiwang Road past Wat Pho towards the city and cross over Sanam Chai Road, you will come to Suan Saranrom → p. 32. To the east of this park is Wat Ratchapradit, a monastery temple which is seldom visited by tourists. It is surrounded by Chinese statues and its doors are exquisitely painted.

The north side of the monastery from Saranrom Road leads to the Pi Kun footbridge (notice the golden pig monument which was erected in 1863 to honour the queen who was born in the year of the pig) which takes you over a canal to the Atsadang Road and to the Wat Ratchabopit → p. 54. The temple is worth visiting for its gates with mother-of-pearl inlays and its towers with flower pattern tiles. On the east side of the monastery is Fungnakorn Road which was once an elephant path and one of the first three roads that were built in Bangkok. Take a left turn here. Shortly before you reach Bamrung Muang Road there is a narrow alley INSIDER TIP Soi Sukha (also Fungnakorn Soi 1) to your right which will take you through an area of picturesque old houses and shops.

When you reach Titong Road, you will see on the other side street Wat Suthat → p. 55. The monastery is famous for its murals and a 14th century statue of Buddha. East of the Wat, in the middle of the Bamrun Muang Road, is the Sao Ching Cha → p. 52, the giant swing. The swing has long been taken down but the red 25m/82ft high construction still represents the courage of the men who risked their lives for a few pennies in the 1930s.

Along the Bamrung Muang Road, and in its side alleys, are lots of shops that sell religious items and the pavements are often full on large statues of golden

Oasis of calm in the old city: a meditative moment in the Wat Suthat temple

Buddhas, wrapped up in plastic. On the eastern corner of the Wat Suthat, where the Unakan Road joins Bamrung Muang Road, is a Hindu shrine in the middle of the traffic island. The Vishnu Mandir is decorated with flower garlands.

Continue further along Bamrung Muang Road and after about 400m you will come to Maha Chai Road. Turn left and you will see Wat Thep Thidaram. This monastery is also off the beaten track. A little bit further is Wat Ratnada → p. 55 which is quite well known but not over crowded. Its main attraction is the Loha Prasat, the Iron Palace.

When you walk further up on Maha Chai Road, you will reach a large intersection. To your left it goes over the Ratchadamnoen Klang Road to the Democracy Monument → p. 34. If you turn right, go over the bridge and immediately turn right again into Boripat Road, and you will then come to the Golden Mount → p. 50. From the top of the 80m/262ft high man-made hill at the monastery Wat Saket, you will have a good lookout point. At the bridge is a pier for the Saen Saep *khlong* boats. For only 12 baht you can now take a cruise up to the Sukhumvit Road (Pier Nana) as a grand finale to your trip. And as you travel along the canal tour you will see that even in the middle of modern Bangkok there are still old wooden stilt houses.

TRAVEL WITH KIDS

Thais love children and many of the better restaurants offer special family events on Sundays which are advertised in the 'Bangkok Post'. **INSIDER TIP** *Kiddy Land (Central World, 6th floor | Ratchadamri Rd | Skytrain: Chit Lom, direct entrance | Budget–Moderate)* is open every day and has restaurants, jungle gyms, children's clothes, carousels and computer games. Kite flying in the middle of a city? In Bangkok the perfect places are Sanam Luang, the large open space in front of the Grand Palace, and in Lumphini Park. Vendors also sell their colourful kites there. Kite flying season is in the windy months – mostly February to the end of April.

BANGKOK DOLL MUSEUM
(123 E5) (*ⓜ K3*)
The exotic dolls here (also for sale) are small works of art and are actually too precious to play with. They are made with loving detail and show, for example, a vegetable seller on a canal boat or mountain people in their splendid costumes. *Mon–Sat 8am–5pm | free admission | 85 Soi Ratchataphan (side street of Ratchaphrarop Rd, north of Prathunam Market) |* *www.bangkokdolls.com | Saen Saep khlong boat: Tha Prathunam | Skytrain: Chit Lom, then 15 minutes on foot*

BENJASIRI PARK (0) (*ⓜ 0*)
Right next door to the Emporium shopping centre. It is a green oasis with a small lake and a fitness track. In the mornings and evenings groups meet here for t'ai chi. The little ones can enjoy the playground and in the evenings you can marvel in wonder at the water fountains that dance with colourful lights to the rhythm of music. The dancing fountain is switched on at 7pm, 7.30pm, 8pm and 8.30pm. *Sukhumvit Rd, Soi 22 | Skytrain: Phrom Phong*

CHILDREN'S DISCOVERY MUSEUM
(0) (*ⓜ 0*)
This interactive museum is designed like a playground. Children can experiment, play music, cook or be firemen here. The museum is situated in the *Queen Sirikit Park*, which is part of *Chatuchak Park*. *Tue–Fri 9am–5pm, Sat/Sun 10am–6pm | admission fee adults 70 baht, children 50 baht | Kamphaeng Pet 4 Rd | www.*

Little explorers will have a great time Bangkok: the city has entertainment activities and playgrounds designed with them in mind

bangkok.com/kids-fun-museums | Skytrain: Mo Chit | MRT: Chatuchak

DREAM WORLD (130 C3) (*⌂ 0*)

The Thai variation of Disneyland: an amusement and theme park with beautiful gardens and the largest slide in Asia. *Nakhon Nayok Rd. Rangsit (province Pathum Thani, about 10 minutes by car north of Don Muang Airport)| www.dreamworld-th.com | Mon–Fri 10am–5pm, Sat/Sun 9am–7pm | admission fee adults/children each 450 baht, toddlers (up to 90 cm) free, some attractions cost extra | Dream World offers lifts to every hotel in Bangkok, return ticket incl. admission ticket and lunch 1000 baht*

DUSIT ZOO (121 E–F 1–2) (*⌂ 0*)

Public zoo with many animals from South East Asia, but also African wildlife like giraffes and lions. With playground, go-cart track, paddle boats and picnic options. *Daily 9am–6pm | admission fee adults 100 baht, children 50 baht | entrances: Rama V Rd, Ratchawithi Rd (main entrance), Uton Nai Rd | Skytrain: Victory Monument, then 10 minutes by taxi*

SIAM OCEAN WORLD ★ ●
(128 A1) (*⌂ H4*)

In South East Asia's biggest shopping centre you will also find its largest aquarium. There are sharks, mantas, penguins and 30,000 other sea creatures. A glass tunnel leads right through the shark pool or explore on a glass bottom boat. And even a walk through a rainforest is an option. Feeding of sharks at 1pm and 4pm, the penguins at midday and 4pm. *Daily 10am–8pm | admission fee adults 850 baht, children 650 baht | Siam Paragon, Rama I Rd | www.siamoceanworld.co.th | Skytrain: Siam Central*

FESTIVALS & EVENTS

Many festivals in Thailand follow the lunar calendar and change every year. The state tourism board, TAT *(www.thailand tourism)* publishes free brochures with the dates every year. You can find a good overview at *www.thailandgrandfestival. com*. On public holidays banks and authorities are closed, but not the exchange counters.

The Buddhist timeline starts with the birth year Buddha. The year 2012 is the Buddhist year 2555.

HOLIDAYS

1 Jan New Year's Day; **full moon in Feb** *Makha Pucha,* commemoration of Buddha's sermon to 1250 followers; **6 April** *Chakri Day,* Rama I's accession, establishment of the Chakri Dynasty in 1782; **12–14 April** *Songkran,* Thai New Year's water festival; **1 May** Workers' Day; **5 May** coronation of King Bhumibol Adulyadej (Rama IX); **full moon in May** *Visakha Pucha,* commemoration of Buddha's birth, enlightenment and death; **full moon in July** *Asaha Pucha,* commemoration of Buddha's first sermon; **the day after Asaha Pucha** *Khaopansa,*

beginning of the Buddhist fast; **12 Aug** Queen Sirikit's birthday; **23 Oct** *Chulalongkorn Day,* anniversary of King Chulalongkorn's death in 1910; **5 Dec** King Bhumibol's birthday; **10 Dec** Constitution Day; **31 Dec** New Year's Eve

FESTIVALS & EVENTS

JANUARY/FEBRUARY
▶ *Chinese New Year's Festival:* Bangkok's Chinatown is an explosion of fireworks and dancing dragons and lions – Chinese operas, many stalls and food stands and *Yaowarat Road* is at the centre of the festivities.

FEBRUARY
▶ *Makha Pucha:* Worshippers encircle Buddhist temples holding lit candles in their hands – the ceremony takes place in Bangkok after sundown at the INSIDER TIP *Wat Benjamaborpit*.

APRIL
▶ *Chakri Day:* Commemorates the founding of the current dynasty and is celebrated with a festival at the *Wat Phra Kaeo*

Parties at full moon: from the New Year water festival to floating bouquets of flowers in November

temple of the Grand Palace. The royal pantheon with its statues of all kings can only be viewed on 6 April.

▶ ★ *Songkran:* No festival is celebrated as enthusiastically as the Thai New Year festival, which takes place from 12 to 14 April (in Chiang Mai to the 15 April). Everyone sprays and pours water on each other, and even tourists get showered. In Bangkok the really wild celebrations are *Patpong* and *Soi Cowboy* as well as in *Khao San Road*, the backpackers area.

MAY

▶ *Royal Ploughing Ceremony:* This splendid spectacle in the second week of May, in front of the *Grand Palace*, marks the beginning of rice growing season. Naturally the royal family has a representative at the event. INSIDER TIP Grandstands for tourists can be booked at the tourist bureau in Bangkok.

NOVEMBER

▶ *Loi Kratong:* The most magical festival of the year, at full moon in November. Baskets filled with flowers, incense and burning candles are placed in the water. The most picturesque area is in Sukhothai and Ayutthaya. In Bangkok the offerings are in honour of the river goddess Mae Kong Ka on the *Chao Phraya*, on canals and on the lake in *Lumphini Park*.

DECEMBER

▶ ★ *Military parade:* Just before the King's birthday the Royal Guard parades in their colourful uniforms at the *Royal Plaza*, in front of the old parliamentary building on Ratchadamnoen Road, and swear allegiance to their king. The parade generally takes place on 3 Dec.

LINKS, BLOGS, APPS & MORE

LINKS

▶ www.bangkok.com/club-guide/club-nights.html There is always a party going on in Bangkok. This site will guide you to the hippest nightclubs with both daily and weekly listing for all the latest happenings

▶ www.bangkok101.com A lifestyle magazine and guide to the latest trends in Bangkok. From shopping to fashion, art and festivals: this is an excellent resource for any visitor to the city

▶ www.thai-blogs.com Richard Barrow is the director of the Paknam Web Network (a collection of English websites about Thailand) and Bangkok's most famous blogger. He tackles a wide range of topics, writes about take-away eateries on the corner as well as the 'cigarette police', who fine tourists when they discard their cigarette butts

BLOGS & FORUMS

▶ www.thaiphotoblogs.com Whether it is Thai royalty or sports, politics or entertainment – Bangkok's events in are captured here

▶ www.bangkokdiaries.com A group blog where anyone can write about their Bangkok impressions and experiences. The topics range from politics through to restaurants and the nightlife

VIDEOS & PODCASTS

▶ www.radiobangkok.net Listen in to the city: Radio Bangkok suggests sightseeing attractions, reports on traffic accidents and makes a declaration of love to the Khao San Road. Also podcasts

▶ www.travelpod.com/videos-mp3s/0/Thailand/Bangkok.html From Chinatown to Thai kick boxing – over 1000 videos about Bangkok

Regardless of whether you are still preparing your trip or already in Bangkok: these addresses will provide you with more information, videos and networks to make your holiday even more enjoyable

▶ www.bangkokpost.com/multimedia/vdo Whether funny and strange or serious and political: for newsworthy happenings in Bangkok, the video reporters of 'Bangkok Post' are there with their cameras

▶ www.5min.com/Video/Visit-The-Grand-Palace-in-Bangkok-Thailand-2372 51173 Have a sneak preview before your trip: this video shows the Grand Palace in its majestic beauty

▶ Bangkok GPS Guide Lost in the city of millions? This iPhone app acts like a compass and shows you where you are, then guides you to your destination

▶ Bangkok Restaurant Finder Use this iPhone app to find that special meal, a free guide to the city's sophisticated restaurants

▶ Lifestyle in Bangkok Hotels, restaurants, shopping, transport – all included in this free App on *www.androidzoom.com*

▶ BKK Transit Go by bus, Skytrain, MRT and *khlong* boat through the metropolis: this free iPhone app is a useful guide to the city's public transport

▶ www.couchsurfing.org Thais and foreigners living in Thailand offer a bed or sofa free of charge on this website

▶ www.hospitalityclub.org Over 600 club members in Bangkok alone. You can spend a night free of charge, get advice or take a walk around the block with them

TRAVEL TIPS

ARRIVAL

✈ Even in high season most national airlines, like British Airways or Thai Airways, have reasonably priced tickets to Bangkok. Low cost airlines are markedly cheaper. For fare comparisons try sites like *www.farecompare.com*, *www.opodo. co.uk* or *www.expedia.com*. International flights arrive at the Suvarnabhumi Airport *(www.airportsuvarnabhumi.com)*.

A ride in the *airport limousine* to the city costs about 1000 baht but you pay less than half of that if you use a public taxi. Cheaper still is the *airport express bus*, which goes to central points in the city and costs about 150 baht.

The quickest way to the city is via the elevated railway line, *Airport Rail Link* (daily 6am–midnight). The Express Line takes you nonstop from the airport to Bangkok City Air Terminal in just 15 minutes for 150 baht (Makkasan Station, from there connection to MRT station Petchaburi). The *City Line* stops at all seven stations between the airport and the final station, Phaya Thai (connection for the Skytrain). The 28km (17mi) takes 30 minutes and the fare to the last station is 45 baht. *Airportraillink.railway.co.th/en/index. html*

🚆 From Singapore you can travel by train across Malaysia to Bangkok (sleeper compartments 2nd class about 2400 baht). Or book the luxurious trip in the Eastern & Oriental Express *(tel. 0221 3 38 03 00 | www.orient-express.com)*.

BANKS & CREDIT CARDS

All banks change traveller's cheques *(Mon– Fri 8.30am–3.30pm | Foreign Exchange counter daily, often until 10pm)* or you can also use your credit card to receive cash in national currency when you show your passport. The easier option is to use your debit or credit card at any of the ATMs. Visa is accepted by all major banks, Mastercard/Eurocard are also widely accepted. With American Express you can only receive cash at Bangkok Bank.

CLIMATE, WHEN TO GO

The majority of tourists come to Bangkok during the peak season which is from November through to February when the temperatures are about 20°C/70°F (at night) to just over 30°C/86°F during the day. By May it is very hot during the day at around 35°C/95°F and at night it is still hot at about 25°C/77°F. During the rainy season from May to October the temperatures decrease a bit more. *www. tmd.go.th/en*

RESPONSIBLE TRAVEL

It doesn't take a lot to be environmentally friendly whilst travelling. Don't just think about your carbon footprint whilst flying to and from your holiday destination but also about how you can protect nature and culture abroad. As a tourist it is especially important to respect nature, look out for local products, cycle instead of driving, save water and much more. If you would like to find out more about eco-tourism please visit: *www.ecotourism.org*

From arrival to weather

Holiday from start to finish: the most important addresses and information for your Bangkok trip

CONSULATES & EMBASSIES

BRITISH EMBASSY
14 Wireless Road | Bangkok 10330 | tel. 0 23 05 83 33 | www.ukinthailand.fco.gov. uk | MRT: Sukhumvit | Mon–Thu 8am–noon, 1–4.30pm, Fri 8am–1pm

AMERICAN EMBASSY
95 Wireless Road | Bangkok 10330 | tel. 0 22 05 40 49 | bangkok.usembassy.gov | Skyytrain: Phloen Chit | Mon–Fri 7.30–11am and 1–2pm

CANADIAN EMBASSY
15th Floor, Abdulrahim Place | 990 Rama IV Road | Bangkok 10500 | tel. 0 26 36 05 40 | www.thailand.gc.ca | MRT: Lumpini | Mon–Thu 7.30am–4.30pm, Fri 7.30am–1pm

BUDGETING

Fruit	40p/¢60	for a mango at a market
Coffee	£1/$1.50	for a cup
Beer	£1.6/$2.40	for a bottle (0.3l) in a bar
T-shirt	£2.80/$4.20	on the steet markets
Taxi	70p/$1	for the first 2km, then 8 baht per km
Soup	70p/$1	at a food stall

CUSTOMS

At arrival, personal items are allowed into the country duty-free, but items worth more than 20,000 US dollars must be declared. The importation of weapons, drugs and pornography is prohibited. You need permission to export Buddha statues, antiques and animal products. Items allowed in the EU: 200 cigarettes or 50 cigars or 250g tobacco, 1L alcohol over than 22% or 2L alcohol under 22%.

ELECTRICITY

The voltage is 220 volts.

EMERGENCY SERVICE

To avoid communication issues it is best to call the tourist police in the event of an emergency. *tel. 1155*

HEALTH

Medical care is excellent and *Bumrungrad* Hospital *(33 Sukhumvit Rd, Soi 3 | tel. 0 26 67 10 00 | www.bumrungrad.com | Skytrain: Nana)* is used by patients from Europe and the USA because treatments here are cheaper than back home. Almost all medicines can be obtained at chemists without a prescription and medicine is also much cheaper than back home. Thais appreciate cleanliness and usually prepare their food under hygienic conditions. You can eat from the food stalls without any concerns. Tap water should only be used to brush your teeth, there are no inoculations required and Bangkok is malaria free.

IMMIGRATION

Citizens of Australia, Canada, Ireland, United Kingdom and the United States of

CURRENCY CONVERTER

£	THB	THB	£
1	50	10	0.20
3	150	30	0.60
5	250	50	1
13	650	130	2.60
40	2000	400	8
75	3750	750	15
120	6000	1200	24
250	12,500	2500	50
500	25,000	5000	100

$	THB	THB	$
1	30	10	0.35
3	90	30	1.05
5	150	50	1.75
13	390	130	4.55
40	1200	400	14
75	2250	750	26.25
120	3600	1200	40
250	7500	2500	87.50
500	12,000	5000	175

For current exchange rates see www.xe.com

America can stay in Thailand without a visa for 30 days (entry by plane) or 15 days (entry over land) for tourism purposes. Your passport has to be valid for a further six months. The tariffs for longer stay visas change constantly so you will need to get this information at embassies and consulates or from their websites.

INFORMATION

TOURIST AUTHORITY OF THAILAND (TAT)
London: *1st Floor, 17–19 Cockspur Street | Trafalgar Square | London SW1Y5BL | tel. 207 9 25 25 11 | www.tourismthailand.org* New York: *61 Broadway, Suite 2810 | New York 10006 | tel. 212 4 32 04 33.* You can find good general information on *www.bang kok.com | www.bangkok.sawadee.com | www.bangkokadvisor.com | www.1stop bangkok.com | www.bangkoktourist.com* and *www.at-bangkok.com.* Detailed maps are found at *www.bangkok-maps.com.*

INFORMATION IN BANGKOK

TOURISM AUTHORITY OF THAILAND (TAT)
The TAT main office is situated on New Phetburi Road *(about five minutes on foot east of the junction of Sukumvit Soi 3 | Mon–Fri 8am–5pm | tel. 0 22 50 55 00 | www.tourismthailand.org)* (0) (𝄞 L4). Information desks are also found at the Ministry of Tourism in the old city *(4 Ratchadamnoen Nok Rd | daily 8.30am–4.30pm)* (121 E4) (𝄞 D2) and at the Arrivals hall in the airport.

BANGKOK TOURIST DIVISION (BTD)
BTD information desks are everywhere in the city. *Daily 9am–7pm | 17/1 Phra Athit Rd (near the National Theatre) | tel. 0 22 25 76 12 | www.bangkoktourist.com* (120 B3) (𝄞 B2)

INTERNET CAFÉS & WIFI

Internet cafés usually charge 1 baht per minute. Many restaurants and most hotels have WiFi hotspots. Many hotels do charge for this service however and it is often a lot more than at an Internet café. If you plan on being online in your hotel first check how much it will cost. You can find hotspot lists online, for example at *www.bkkpages. com/useful/wifi/free-of-charge.*

MEDIA

English newspapers are the 'Bangkok Post' and 'The Nation'.

PHONE & MOBILE PHONE

In Thailand you also dial the area code when dialling locally, in Bangkok it is *02* (included in the numbers in this guide). If you are calling Thailand from overseas, the dialling code is *0066* plus the local dialling code without zero, so to Bangkok it is *00662*.

If you have taken your cell phone with you, it will automatically connect with your service provider's Thai network partner. Roaming is very expensive. Even if someone calls you from overseas, you will pay for the majority of the phone call. Calling from a hotel can also be very expensive.

Most reasonable option is to use a Thai SIM card using your own (this only works if your phone is not blocked from using other SIM cards). These rechargeable cards are available at many stalls and at all *7-Eleven* shops. A call to the UK costs about 20 baht per minute. If you dial the cheap dialling code *007*, *008* or *009* instead of *001*, you can call for less than 10 baht.

Thai service providers are increasingly providing more country dialling codes with various tariffs and quality. *True Move* offers calls to the UK via the Internet with the dialling code *00600* from only 1 baht per minute. The three large companies are AIS, *(www.ais.co.th/12call/en/index. html)*, DTAC *(www.happy.co.th/home_ en.php)* and *True Move (www.truemove. com/en/Inter-SIM-Prepay.rails)*.

You can also call free of charge: from Skype to Skype *(www.skype.com)* at an Internet café or on your own laptop.

POST

An example of the cost for postage: an airmail letter to Europe (up to 10g) costs

USEFUL PHRASES THAI

Letters in *italics* (masculine form) are to be replaced by the respective feminine form *[...]*, as necessary.

Yes/No	*krap [kah]* chai/mai chai	ครับ(ค่ะ) ใช่/ไม่ใช่
Please/Thank you	khaw ... noy/khop koon *krab [kah]*	ขอ...หน่อย/ขอบคุณครับ(ค่ะ)
Sorry	khaw toht	ขอโทษ !
Good afternoon!/evening!	sahwadee *krab [kah]*	สวัสดีครับ(ค่ะ)
Goodbye	sahwadee	สวัสดี !
My name is ...	chan joo ...	ฉันชื่อ ...
I'm from ...	chan ma jag ...	ฉันมาจาก ......
I don't understand you	chan mai khao jai koon	ฉันไม่เข้าใจคุณ
How much is ...?	nee laka taolai	นี่ราคาเท่าไร ?
Excuse me, where can I find ...?	khaw toht *krab [kah]* ... yuu tee nai	ขอโทษครับ(ค่ะ) ... อยู่ที่ไหน ?

1 nueng	หนึ่ง	5 hah	ห้า	9 gao	เก้า
2 song	สอง	6 hok	หก	10 sip	สิบ
3 sahm	สาม	7 jet	เจ็ด	20 yee sip	ยี่สิบ
4 see	สี่	8 beht	แปด	100 nueng loi	หนึ่งร้อย

17 baht, postcards 15 baht. They take about five days to arrive.

PRICES & CURRENCY

The Thai baht is divided into 100 satang. Coins of 1, 2, 5 and 10 baht as well as notes of 20, 50, 100, 500 and 1000 baht are in circulation. You will only get 25 and 50 satang coins as change in supermarkets, also calculate the prices after the comma. Prices in Bangkok vary tremendously: for the price of a cappuccino in a tourist café on Sukhumvit Road you can get an entire meal at a restaurant in Chinatown.

PUBLIC TOILETS

Public toilets can be found all over Bangkok in the shopping mall, parks, lobbies of hotels and restaurants. They vary from western style to the local style and have different standards of cleanliness but most of the large shopping centres and hotels have spotless facilities. Keep some small coins on hand as some facilities do charge.

PUBLIC TRANSPORT

BOAT

Express boats travel to and fro on the Chao Phraya. There are also ferries at the piers (Tha) crossing the river to Thonburi while *khlongs*, the canal boats, travel across Bangkok on the Saen Saep canal *(www. chaophrayaboat.co.th)*.

BUS

Fleets of private and public busses travel through the city. A city plan showing the bus routes is available at the Tourism Authority of Thailand (TAT) free of charge or at a bookstore. The site *www.bmta. co.th/en/travel.php* lists all the public bus routes with their numbers and bus stops.

MRT

The Mass Rapid Transit goes from the Central Station Hua Lamphong via Silom Road (connection to the Skytrain station Sala Daeng) and Sukhumvit Road (connection to the Skytrain station Asok) all the way to Chatuchak Weekend Market. The fare is 40 baht max. You can also get a Day Pass for 120 baht. *www.bangkok metro.co.th*

SKYTRAIN (BTS)

The overhead railway is Bangkok's best mode of transport (daily 6am–midnight in five minute intervals). Three routes take you to the north up to Chatuchak Park, to the south over King Taksin Bridge/ Chao Phraya, to the east up to the final station On Nut at Sukhumvit Road (Soi 77). Transfer station at Siam Square. Tickets cost between 10 and 40 baht depending on zone, the Day Pass costs 120 baht. *www.bts.co.th*

TAXI & TUK-TUK

Almost all taxis have meters but make sure that the driver turns it on before you drive off. The first 2km costs 35 baht, all consecutive ones 5.50 baht. Hardly any of the drivers speak English, but they all know the names of the larger hotels. Get someone from the hotel to write down your other destinations in Thai for you. The tuk-tuk is a three-wheeled motorbike rickshaw. Bargain with your driver beforehand and agree on a price. The drive will generally be more expensive than a taxi. But you should not pay more than 100 baht for a tour around the city.

TAX REFUNDS

The larger shops, restaurants and hotels add 7% VAT onto the bill but this is not necessarily the case with the smaller shops. You can get your tax back on departure, if you have goods (not gemstones!) worth at least 5000 baht in shops that show VAT Refund for Tourists, if you have your passport with you and if you have the correct forms and have spent at least 2000 baht at each shop. Goods and the respective invoices need to be presented to the VAT Refund Office at the airport. *www.rd.go.th/vrt*

TIME

Indochina Time (ICT) is seven hours ahead of Greenwich Mean Time (GMT), during European summer plus six hours, fifteen hours behind US Eastern Time (EST) and four hours behind Australian Eastern Time (AEST), one hour less during summers daylight saving time.

TIPPING

In simple establishments or food stalls it is not common to tip. The better restaurants include a service charge of 10 per cent. Only tip if the service was exceptional. In restaurants without a service charge, but with friendly service, a 10 per cent tip is appropriate. Many hotels also add a service charge for the room. Nevertheless, the hotel personnel appreciate tips. It is not common practice to tip taxi drivers.

WEATHER IN BANGKOK

	Jan	Feb	March	April	May	June	July	Aug	Sept	Oct	Nov	Dec
Daytime temperatures in °C/°F	32/90	33/91	34/93	35/95	34/93	33/91	32/90	32/90	32/90	31/88	31/88	31/88
Nighttime temperatures in °C/°F	20/68	23/73	24/75	26/79	25/77	25/77	25/77	24/75	24/75	24/75	23/73	20/68
Sunshine hours/day	8	8	8	10	8	6	5	5	5	6	7	8
Precipitation days/month	1	2	3	4	13	14	15	15	17	13	4	1
Water temperatures in °C/°F	26/79	27/81	27/81	28/82	28/82	28/82	28/82	28/82	28/82	27/81	27/81	27/81

NOTES

MARCO POLO TRAVEL GUIDES

ALGARVE
AMSTERDAM
AUSTRALIA
BANGKOK
BARCELONA
BERLIN
BRUSSELS
BUDAPEST
CALIFORNIA
CAPE TOWN
  WINE LANDS,
  GARDEN ROUTE
COLOGNE
CORFU
GRAN CANARIA
CRETE
CUBA
CYPRUS
  NORTH AND
  SOUTH
DUBAI

DUBROVNIK &
  DALMATIAN COAST
EDINBURGH
EGYPT
FINLAND
FLORIDA
FRENCH RIVIERA
  NICE, CANNES &
  MONACO
HONGKONG
  MACAU
IRELAND
ISRAEL
ISTANBUL
JORDAN
KOS
LAKE GARDA

LANZAROTE
LAS VEGAS
LONDON
LOS ANGELES
MADEIRA
  PORTO SANTO
MALLORCA
MALTA
  GOZO
MOROCCO
NEW YORK
NEW ZEALAND
NORWAY
PARIS
RHODES

ROME
SAN FRANCISCO
SICILY
SOUTH AFRICA
STOCKHOLM
TENERIFE
THAILAND
TURKEY
  SOUTH COAST
UNITED ARAB
  EMIRATES
VENICE
VIETNAM

- PACKED WITH INSIDER TIPS
- BEST WALKS AND TOURS
- FULL-COLOUR PULL-OUT MAP
  AND STREET ATLAS

STREET ATLAS

The green line ▭ indicates the Walking tours (p. 98–103)

All tours are also marked on the pull-out map

Photo: Silom District, Skytrain station Chong Nonsi

D

Tao Hao
Ratcha Kru
Housing Estate

Isan Bag
Factory

E

Sol

Phahonyothin

3

Phahonyothin

F

1

★ 10

Building

400 m

437 yd

Thai
ange

Housing
Estate of the
Police

Sanam Pao

Phaya Thai 2
Hospital

Pratueang Suk
Women's Houses

Thanon

TV Channel 587

Akkawimon

Bunchusi

Bunyu

oke-Rachadapisek

hao
tate

Bank
of Asia

Soi
Phahonyothin

Sa Nam Rhao

Phra Mang

Saeng Tawi Flats

Ampawanmit

Ruanmit

2

Wat Aphai
Thayaram

Thanon

31

withi
sp

Siam
City Bank

Children's
Hosp
Anutsawari
Chaisamoraphum
(Victory Monument)

People's
Dept Store

Robinson
Dept Store

Siam Comm.
Bank

Expressway

Din Daeng

Min. of
Labour
Soc.

3

ry Monument

Phaya Thai

Yothi

Ratchawithi

Loei Panya

Wattanavithi

Chaisamoraphum

Santi

Phab

Sukhabobusang

Soi

Wat Taohan

Bangkok
Bank

Soi Thalad

Chalerm-Mahanakhon-Expressway

Thai Thip

Rong Rian Rapprasong

Sri Din Dang
Market

Thanon

S Phra San Sarp

Thanon

Yothi

Thanon

Soi Chawakun

Soi Alam

Songklo

Soi

Bangkok
Metropolitan
Park

Rang Nam

Soi
Ratchaprarop

Bunprarop

Ratchaprarop

Ratchateophan

Klong Samsen

4

7

Express Transit
Organization

Thephatsadin

Ratchaprarop

Soi Ratchatsuhan

Makkasan
Market

Makkasan
Interchange

Porn Prom
Appartm.
Bldg

Express Transportation
Organization

Soi Polalit

Soi Ayudhaya

Krung Thai
Bank

Sri-Ayudhaya

Decha
Hosp

Suan Pakkard
Palace

Phaya Thai
t Station

Thai-Nat'l
Organization
for Nervous
Diseases

Phaya
Thai 1 Hosp

Makkasan
Small
Electricity Stat.

Baiyoke II Tower
Ratchaprarop
Railway Station

Makkasan Railway
Station

Church of
Christ

Phetburi 11

Phetburi

Phetburi

Soi

Soi
Wutthi
Pan

Nat'l Youth Bureau

Thanon

Ind. Estatr Auth.
of Thailand

Wattanawong

Phetburi 31

Ghalerm-

5

ประตูน้ำ

PRATHUNAM

Baiyoke
Tower

Soi Phetburi 21

Soi
Phetburi

Pratunam
Market

Dental
Clinic

City Dept.
Store

Makkasan
Market

Wattanasin
Trammarot
Fresh Market

Phetburi 33

Metro
Dept
Store

Phetburi 35

ressway

Pantip
Plaza

Chalermlok
Market

S.Ph.22

S.Ph.24

Platinum
S.C.

Soi Samy
ran

Women's
Appartm.

Hatsadin

Phetbури

Thanon

Phetburi

Soi San
Phetburi 25

S. Phetburi 23

S.Phetburi 27

S.Phetburi 29

Siam City
Bank

Phetburi

Phetburi 37

Phetburi
Hosp.

Soi

9 ★

★ 14

i

tral

Wat Pathum
Wanaran

Central
World
Plaza

Ratcha

Phrasing

Ratchadamri

Soi
Phetburi

Tha-Pratumnam

Klong San Sap

Tha-Chit-Lom

Siam Comm. Bank

Chitlom

Withayu

6

Siam Ocean

Big C
Shopping
Center

Aroma
Hotel

Nara

S.Ratc

123

Siam Pen
House IV

Chitlom
Plastic Surgery
Hospital

The
Promenade
Shopping Center

128

SIAM SQUARE

123 9 14 B

Siam Discovery Ctr
Siam Paragon
Siam Central
Wat Pathum Wanaran
Siam Ocean World

Central World Plaza

Arnoma Hotel
Narai Phand
S.Ratchadamri
Th. Gesq.
Gaysorn Plaza

C

Siam Pen House IV
Telephone Organisation of Thailand

Wongwian Pathumwan Thanon
Thanon Phaya-Thai

Rama 1
Thanon
Chit Lom

Soi
Siam Square 9
Siam Square 7
Siam Square 5
Siam Square 3
Siam Square 1

Henri Dunant

National Police Department
General Police Hosp.

Erawan Shrine
Maneeya Ctr D.S.
Amarin Plaza S.C.
Lang Suan

Central Chit Lo. D.S.

Chulalongkorn 64
Siam Square

ปทุมวัน
PATHUMWAN

Ratchadamri

Peninsula Plaza
Soi Mahat Lek Luang 1

Soi Bahn Lang Suan

Chulalongkorn 62
Uthenthawai Technological School

Royal

Soi Mahat Lek Luang 2

Soi Lang Suan 1

2

Pathumwan Sinaicha Rintharawirot University

Bangkok

Soi Mahat Lek Luang 3

Soi Lang Suan 2

Mura Building

Ratchadamri

S.L.Suan 1

National History Museum
-ing Technology Museum

Sportclub

S.L.Suan 3
S.L.Suan 4

Chulalongkorn

Ambassador Court

S.L.Suan 5

University

Charoe Court Building

S.L.Suan 6
Soi Lang Suan 7

Si B

3

The Thai Red Cross Society

Pathumwan Waterworks

Big Office Building
Soi

Sara

Chulalongkorn 60
S.Chu. 58
Chulalongkorn 56

Pasteur Institute (Snake Farm)

Chulalongkorn

Lumphini Park

Thanon
-ump
Soi
Montien Plaza
Surawong
Wallstreet Tower
Patpong Night Market
Robinson D.S.

Chulalongkorn Hospital

Silom
Wongwian Sala Daeng
King Rama VI Monument

(Suan Lumphini)

4

15

Jim Thompson's Thai Silk
Bangkok Christian Hosp
Liberty Square

Silom
Sala Daeng
Silom Complex
Silom Sala Daeng 2

Rama-IV
Wongwian Witthayu

Thanon
Bangkok Bank
Big Office Building

BNH Hospital

Soi Sala Daeng
Soi Yommarat
Sala Daeng 2

Hongkong Bank
Sala Daeng 2

Cathay Trust Bldg.
Satorn Nuea
Lump

5

Trinity Complex
Silom 3
Phiphat 2
President House
Phiphat 1

Trinity Hall Church
Soi Chong Rak Morlat
Convent

Thai Wah Tower

Community of Y.M.C.A.

S

Division for Asylants
City Bank
Soi Pilin

Thanon
Munity for the Americans
Soi Tri Thai Chiang
Munity
Soi Tanasin
S.Suan Phlu 2
Huayon

Nantha
Big Office Buildin

6

Empire Tower
Naradhiwas Rajanagarindra

สาธร
SATORN

Soi Suan Phlu 1
Soi Prasart Court

Munity of Thammasat University

Bhirasi of Modern

Naradhiwas Rajanagarindra

Immigration Dept

400 m
437 yd

128

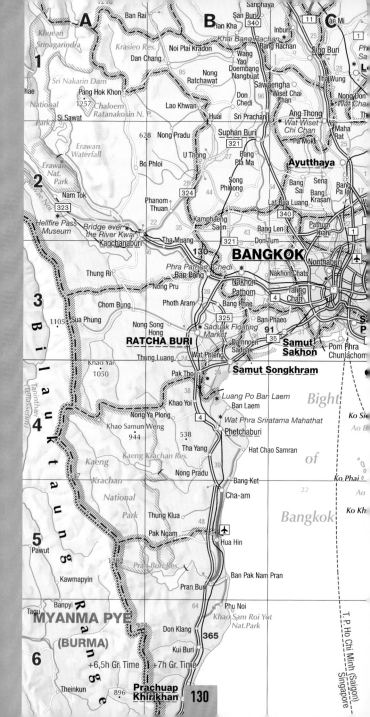

Khuean
Srinagarindra

Ban Rai

San Buri

Sanphaya

Inburi

Ban Kha

A 340 **B** Khai Bang Rachan **C** 11 Ban Mi

Bang Rachan

Noi Plai Kradon

Sing Buri

ThaWung

Nong Chai
Wat Cha

Krasieo Res.

Dan Chang

Wang Yao
Doembang
Nangbuat

Sawaengha

1

Sri Nakarin Dam

95

Nong Ratchawat

Don Chedi

Wiset Chai Chan

96

Pang Hok Khon

1257 Chaloem Ratanakosin N. P.

Lao Kwan

Huai

Sri Prachan

Ang Thong

Wat Wiset Chi Chan

Maha Rat

Si Sawat

National
Park

628 Nong Pradu

U Thong

321

Suphan Buri

Pa'Mok

25

Erawan
Waterfall

Bang Pla Ma

Ayutthaya

Erawan
Nat.
Park

Bo Phloi

Song Phimong

Bang Sai

Sena

Bang Pa In

2

Nam Tok

324

44

54

Lat Bua Luang

Bang Krasan

17

323

Phanom Thuan

Kamphaeng Saen

340

Bang Len

Pathum Thani

Hellfire Pass
Museum

Bridge over
the River Kwai

22

35

Don Tum

321

Kanchanaburi

Tha Muang

130

Don Tum

1

66

BANGKOK

Phra Pathom Chedi

Nonthaburi

Thung Ri

Ban Pong

Nakhon Chats

Nong Pru

Nakhon Pathom

3

Chom Bung

Photh Aram

Bang Phae

4

Taling Chan

1105 Sua Phung

325

Ban Phaeo

91

Nong Song Hong

Saduak Floating Market

36

35

Samut
Sakhon

RATCHA BURI

Damnoen Saduak

Samut

Pom Phra
Chunlachom

Thung Luang

Wat Phleng

Khao Yai
1050

Pak Tho

24

Samut Songkhram

38

Khao Yoi

Luang Po Ban Laem

Ban Laem

Bight

Nong Ya Plong

4

Wat Phra Sriratama Mahathat

Ko Si

Khao Samun Weng
944

538

Phetchaburi

Ao B

4

Tha Yang

Hat Chao Samran

of

Kaeng Krachan Res.

Nong Pradu

39

Bang Ket

Ko Phai

Ko Kh

Kaeng
Krachan

National

Park

Cha-am

22

Ao

Bangkok

Thung Klua

48

5

Pak Ngam

Hua Hin

Pawut

Pran Buri Res.

Kawmapyin

Ban Pak Nam Pran

Pran Buri

64

Banpyi

Phu Noi

Tagu

Khao Sam Roi Yot
Nat.Park

MYANMA PYE

Don Klang

365

(BURMA)

+6,5h Gr. Time +7h Gr. Time

6

Kui Buri

Theinkun

896

**Prachuap
Khirikhan**

130

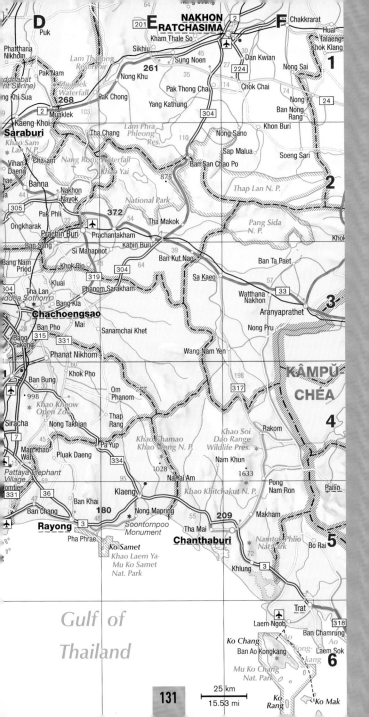

This index lists a selection of the streets and squares shown in the street atlas

KEY TO STREET ATLAS

ทางหลวงแผ่นดิน Autobahn		Motorway Autoroute	
ถนนสี่เลน Vierspurige Straße		Road with four lanes Route à quatre voies	
ถนนเชื่อมระหว่างเมือง Durchgangsstraße		Thoroughfare Route de transit	
ถนนสายเอก Hauptstraße		Main road Route principale	
ถนนอื่นๆ Sonstige Straßen		Other roads Autres routes	
สถานที่บริการคำแนะนำ Information		Information Information	
ทางวันเวย์ – สถานที่จอดรถ Einbahnstraße - Parkplatz		One-way street - Parking place Rue à sens unique - Parking	
ทางรถไฟพร้อมสถานีรถไฟ Hauptbahn mit Bahnhof		Main railway with station Chemin de fer principal avec gare	
ทางของรถอื่นๆที่ใช้ราง Sonstige Bahn		Other railway Autre ligne	
ทางรถบัส Buslinie mit Endhaltestelle		Bus-route with terminus Ligne d'autobus avec terminus	
โบสถ์ – สุเหร่า Kirche - Moschee		Church - Mosque Église - Mosquée	
ศาลเจ้า Schrein		Shrine Châsse	
วัด – วัดที่ท่าชม Tempel - Sehenswerter Tempel		Temple - Temple of interest Temple - Temple remarquable	
ที่พักเยาวชน – โรงพยาบาล Jugendherberge - Krankenhaus		Youth hostel - Hospital Auberge de jeunesse - Hôpital	
อนุสาวรีย์ – หอสูง Denkmal - Turm		Monument - Tower Monument - Tour	
ตำรวจ – หอส่งสัญญาณ Polizeistation - Funkturm		Police station - Radio tower Poste de police - Tour radio	
ไปรษณีย์ – ท่าจอดเรือ Postamt - Anlegestelle		Post office - Landing stage Bureau de poste - Embarcadère	
สถานที่ก่อสร้าง Bebaute Fläche		Built-up area Zone bâtie	
ตึกต่างๆของทางราชการ Öffentliches Gebäude		Public building Bâtiment public	
เขตอุตสาหกรรม Industriegelände		Industrial area Zone industrielle	
สวนพักผ่อน ป่า – สุสานมุสลิม Park, Wald - Moslemischer Friedhof		Park, forest - Muslim cemetery Parc, bois - Cimetière musulman	
เขตเมือง Stadtgrenze		Municipal boundary Limite municipale	
เดินเล่นในเมือง Stadtspaziergänge		Walking tours Promenades en ville	
MARCO POLO Highlight		MARCO POLO Highlight	

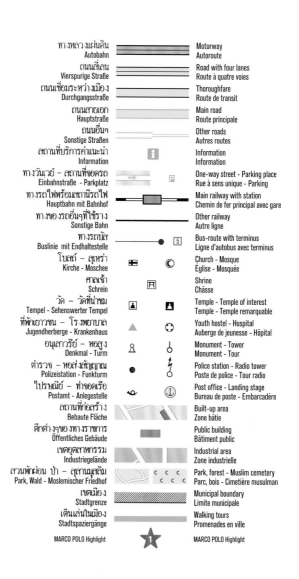

INDEX

This index lists all places, sights and museums featured in this guide
Numbers in bold indicate a main entry

WRITE TO US

e-mail: info@marcopologuides.co.uk

Did you have a great holiday? Is there something on your mind? Whatever it is, let us know! Whether you want to praise, alert us to errors or give us a personal tip – MARCO POLO would be pleased to hear from you. We do everything we can to provide the very latest information for your trip.

Nevertheless, despite all of our authors' thorough research, errors can creep in. MARCO POLO does not accept any liability for this. Please contact us by e-mail or post.

MARCO POLO Travel Publishing Ltd Pinewood, Chineham Business Park Crockford Lane, Chineham Basingstoke, Hampshire RG24 8AL United Kingdom

PICTURE CREDITS
Cover photograph: Grand Palace and Chao Phraya (Laif/hemis.fr: Boisvieux)
The Anna Restaurant & Art Gallery (16 top); DuMont Bildarchiv: Sasse (3 top, 68/69, 85); © fotolia.com: Kzenon (16 bottom); Greyhound Co., Ltd.: Chutharut Pornmuneesoontorn (16 centre); W. Hahn (1 bottom, 24 top, 63, 75, 87); Huber: Huber (3 bottom, 88/89), Picture Finder (18/19), Schmid (50); © istockphoto.com: tbradford (17 bottom); V. E. Janicke (36/37, 42, 108 bottom); R. Junge (22/23); M. Kirchgessner (60, 64 left, 108 top, 109); G. Knoll (73); Laif: Henseler (21), Heuer (front flap right, 2 bottom, 32/33, 41, 47, 56/57), Linkel (24 bottom, 93), Sasse (3 centre, 55, 80/81); Laif/hemis.fr: Boisvieux (1 top), Gardel (2 top, 5); H. Leue (7, 52); K. Maeritz (15, 104/105); mauritius images: Alamy (2 centre top, 6, 70, 90, 95, 103), Beck (106/107), Lescourret (25); The Metropolitan, Bangkok (17 top); A. M. Mosler (77); M. Sasse (8, 9, 10/11, 107, 137); A. Sperber (30, 106); O. Stadler (38, 58, 64 right, 82, 98/99, 105, 118/119); T. Stankiewicz (front flap left, 2 centre bottom, 4, 12/13, 26/27, 49, 53, 65, 66); vario images: RHPL (34); Visum: Grieshaber (78, 104); White Star: Schiefer (101)

1st Edition 2013
Worldwide Distribution: Marco Polo Travel Publishing Ltd, Pinewood, Chineham Business Park, Crockford Lane, Basingstoke, Hampshire RG24 8AL, United Kingdom. Email: sales@marcopolouk.com
© MAIRDUMONT GmbH & Co. KG, Ostfildern
Chief editors: Michaela Lienemann (concept, managing editor), Marion Zorn (concept, text editor)
Author: Wilfried Hahn; editor: Corinna Walkenhorst
Programme supervision: Ann-Katrin Kutzner, Nikolai Michaelis, Silwen Randebrock
Picture editors: Gabriele Forst, Stefan Scholtz
What's hot: wunder media, München
Cartography street atlas: © MAIRDUMONT, Ostfildern; Cartography pull-out map: © MAIRDUMONT, Ostfildern
Design: milchhof: atelier, Berlin; Front cover, pull-out map cover, page 1: factor product munich
Translated from German by Nicole Meyer; editor of the English edition: Margaret Howie, fullproof.co.za
Prepress: M. Feuerstein, Wigel

DOS & DON'TS ☝

Beware of throwing away cigarette butts or insulting the king

DO NOT GET MIXED UP WITH DRUG DEALERS

If you are found with drugs, you can count on dire consequence, possibly the death penalty. Even small amounts of *ganja* (marijuana) can land you in prison. Just keep moving if someone offers you *ganja* in tourist centres like Khao San Road. Dealers sometimes blow the whistle on their clients.

DO HAVE SMALL CHANGE FOR THE TAXI

Drivers may say, 'Unfortunately I don't have any small change' and so try to con you into giving them a tip. The same applies to getting on to a bus without small change. The conductor takes payment during the ride, and it has to take place quickly. If you produce a large note, it can take time and you might even miss your stop.

DO NOT INSULT THE ROYAL FAMILY

Criticising the monarchy is taboo in Thailand and the rule also applies to foreigners. In 2009 the Australian author Harry Nicolaides was sentenced to three years imprisonment because he was critical of the Crown Prince in a book. The king pardoned him after a few weeks, but Nicolaides was held for six months awaiting trial.

DO AVOID THE TOUTS

There are taxi drivers and tuk-tuk drivers who offer sightseeing tours for free or for a special price. But the tour can cost you more than you bargained for. The driver gets commissions from the stores he takes you to. And stores that work with them specialise in ripping off customers. There are also touts that roam around disguised as friendly passers-by at all the important sightseeing attractions (especially near the Grand Palace). They lurk about and wait for their next victim, the usual ploy is to tell you that the palace is shut due to a holiday, but they would be happy to show you some other sightseeing attractions. This tour will certainly take you to shady businesses. Rule of thumb: Thais are generally reserved and will not speak to strangers on the street. More info about tourist incidents can be found at *www.bangkokscams.com*.

DO NOT LITTER

Do not drop anything on street, not even a cigarette butt. The city council has warning signs everywhere and littering is strictly monitored with hefty fines of up to 2000 baht – especially in the tourist districts. The belief that 'rich' tourists are targeted cannot be denied. But that is not going to help you if you do get caught.